The Web of Belief

Consulting Editor / *Richard Ohmann*
WESLEYAN UNIVERSITY

THE WEB
OF BELIEF

by W. V. Quine *Harvard University*

J. S. Ullian *Washington University*

 RANDOM HOUSE   NEW YORK

Contents

The Web of Belief

Chapter I

Belief and
Change of Belief

Most of us believe that Hannibal crossed the Alps, that Neptune is a planet, that frozen foods thaw when left at room temperature overnight. We also share beliefs of higher order—beliefs about our beliefs. We all hold, for example, that those gained from respected encyclopedias and almanacs are much more to be relied on than those gained from television commercials. Further, we agree that what we think we see is, much more often than not, genuinely there. Seeing is not quite believing, but it, together with the continual "testimony" of our other senses, fairly bombards us with new material that requires assimilation in our body of belief. So it is that each of us is continually adopting new beliefs, rejecting old ones, and questioning still others. One's repertoire of beliefs changes at least slightly in nearly every waking moment, since the merest chirp of a bird or chug of a passing motor, when recognized as such, adds a belief—however trivial and temporary—to our fluctuating store.

And yet, for all the liveliness of fluctuation of beliefs, believing is not itself an activity. It is not like scansion or long division. Nor is it a fit or mood, like joy or grief or astonishment. It is not something that we feel while it lasts. Rather, believing is a disposition that can linger latent and unobserved. It is a disposition to respond in certain ways when the appropriate issue arises. To believe that Hannibal crossed the Alps is to be disposed, among other things, to say "Yes" when asked. To believe that frozen foods will thaw on the table is to be disposed, among other things, to leave such foods on the table only when one wants them thawed.

Inculcating a belief is like charging a battery. The battery is thenceforward disposed to give a spark or shock, when suitably approached, as long as the charge lasts; similarly the believer is disposed to respond in characteristic ways, when suitably approached, as long as the belief lasts. The belief, like the charge, may last long or briefly. Some beliefs, like the one about Hannibal, we shall probably retain while we live. Some, like our belief in the dependability of our neighborhood cobbler, we may abandon tomorrow in the face of adverse evidence. And some, like the belief that a bird chirped within earshot, will simply die of unimportance forthwith. The belief that the cobbler is dependable gives way tomorrow to a contrary belief, while the belief in the bird is just forgotten. A disposition has ceased in both cases, though in different ways.

We often talk as if believing were something that a man does *to* something: to some intangible thing which is *what* he believes. To name this thing we enlist a sentence as subordinate clause. For example, we speak of the belief *that* Hannibal crossed the Alps and *that* Neptune is a planet. We use a sentence, with "that" prefixed, as a name of the "thing" believed. Now what manner of thing is this believed thing—*that* Hannibal crossed the Alps? To say that it is just the sentence itself seems mistaken. Foreign speakers, after all, are said to share the belief that Hannibal crossed the Alps, even when they do not understand the English sentence. We also like to attribute a belief to a dumb animal, on the strength of his dispositions. So with the dog who wags his tail at the sound of a car in the driveway. And we sometimes even like to distinguish two beliefs when the sentence is one; for instance, the sentence "I am Napoleon" expresses different beliefs about Napoleon when uttered by different patients. Therefore, one tends to conclude that the things believed are not the sentences themselves. What then are they?

This, like various other philosophical questions, is better deflected than met head on. Instead of worrying about the simple verb "believes" as relating men to some manner of believed things, we can retreat to the word-pair "believes true" as relating men directly to sentences. We can retreat to this without claiming that believed things are sentences; we can simply waive that claim, and the philosophical question behind it. After all, our factual interest in what some speaker of English believes is fully satisfied by finding out what sentences he believes to be true.

And what criterion have we for saying that a man believes a sentence to be true? For most purposes the criterion is the obvious one: the man assents to the sentence when asked. The criterion can fail if the man does not understand our language, or if he chooses to deceive us. Also the criterion is inadequate to the purposes of a psychiatrist who wants to provide for some manner of unapprehended belief or disbelief. But it is perhaps criterion enough for us.

To be quite exact, "believes true" should be seen as relating men not to sentences but to individual acts of sentence utterance. For, as illustrated by "I am Napoleon" or "The door is open," one utterance of a sentence can be true and another false. In general, however, it is easier to specify a sentence, simply by quoting it, than to specify some individual act of utterance. So let us continue to speak simply of sentences as true and as believed true, except where confusion threatens.

For that matter, where no confusion threatens, it will be convenient and natural to go on speaking even in the old way of what a man believes, instead of what he believes true. But whenever we are threatened by the philosophical question of objects of belief, we can gratefully retreat to the more explicit idiom which speaks of believing sentences true, or, ultimately, of believing utterances true.

It is important to distinguish between disbelief and nonbelief— between believing a sentence false and merely not believing it true. Disbelief is a case of belief; to believe a sentence false is to believe the negation of the sentence true. Nonbelief is the state of suspended judgment: neither believing the sentence true nor believing it false. This is nothing so cantankerous as believing the sentence to be neither true nor false; on the contrary, it is simply the absence of opinion.

English usage is perverse on the point: we say, confusingly, the weaker "I don't believe so" to mean the stronger "I believe not." But the fact is, taking any sentence at random, that belief and disbelief are less usual than nonbelief. Are there an even number of Paul Smiths in Boston? Will it rain in Pontiac next

Labor Day? English being what it is, we answer "I don't know," because it would be misleading to say "I don't believe so." But our state is simple nonbelief.

The flight to "I don't know" compounds the perversity of idiom, for knowing is quite a special kind of believing; you can believe without knowing. Believing something does not count as knowing it unless what is believed is in fact true. And even if what is believed is true, believing it does not count as knowing it unless the believer is aware of very dependable grounds for his belief.

Another irregularity of English usage is a hyperbolic use of "know" as an emphatic variant of "believe." "I know the tornado will hit us," uttered with a shudder, might reflect maximum fear on minimum evidence. Knowledge soberly so-called, on the other hand, is belief at its soberest, farthest from speculation. Knowledge is a laudable aspiration, and speculation is laudable too as long as we are aware of what we are doing. And between these termini, inclusive, there stretches our whole fluctuating spectrum of beliefs.

Though many of our beliefs are here to stay, at other points the body of our beliefs is, we noted, perpetually in flux. Primarily this is because our senses keep adding information. This simple addition of information, at the sensory end, issues in change in the body of beliefs that is not to be equated with simple addition of beliefs. For one thing, beliefs get crowded out and are simply forgotten. This happens promptly to the host of trivialities such as the chirp of the bird and the chug of the motor. For another thing, more to the point of our study, beliefs still vigorously present and not to be forgotten can come into conflict with the new arrivals and be forced from the field. Sometimes, sad to say, we do go on assenting to sentences that contradict one another, but this is because inconsistency is not always obvious. We can no longer believe all of a set of sentences to be true once we know them to be in contradiction with one another, since contradiction requires one or another of them to be false.

A person need never have questioned his evidence for anything in order to be rich in opinion. On the contrary. Once he recognizes a conflict among his beliefs, however, it is up to him to gather and assess his evidence with a view to weeding out one or another of the conflicting beliefs.

Evidence for belief must be distinguished from causes of belief. Often we gather evidence to defend a belief that we already hold, while the cause of our already having held the belief is forgotten or undiscovered. Sounds in the night that are not even consciously detected may contribute to our beliefs. We may have come in this way to believe that our fraternity brother got back from his revels; yet, the first evidence we are in a position to cite for the belief may come only the next morning when we see his sports car in the drive.

What we call hunches from out of nowhere probably spring from unnoticed stimulations. Moreover, beliefs that we think ourselves to have adopted by reflection alone may well have had other causes. Our fears and hopes can affect our beliefs, and probably for all of us do. But our fears and hopes are not part of the evidence for what we believe. Indeed one obvious test that must be passed by evidence is this: Would it still be taken to support the belief in question if we stripped away all motives for wanting that belief to be true? Probably few of us would offer as evidence anything failing this test; yet probably all of us hold some beliefs that would be seen to lack support if this standard were judiciously applied.

As long as a belief whose causes are undetected is not challenged by other persons, and engenders no conflict that would prompt us to wonder about it ourselves, we are apt to go on holding it without thought of evidence. This practice is often reasonable, time being limited. But it remains important to keep in mind that cause is not evidence, for this keeps us on the alert for any hint that the time has come when the evidence for one of our beliefs should be sought and sifted. By keeping this in mind we diminish, moreover, our susceptibility to some of the causes of belief which have nothing to do with evidence, such as the catchiness of an advertising jingle.

The intensity of a belief cannot be counted on to reflect its supporting evidence any more than its causes can. We may have little support for a belief tightly held, or much support for a belief the inference to which we have not yet made. So the story of the origins and intensities of our beliefs, the story of what happens in our heads, is a very different story from the one sought in the quest for evidence. Where we are rational in our beliefs the stories may correspond; elsewhere they diverge. The former story is for psychology to tell. On the other hand, our present concern is with grounds, with reasons, with the evidential relations that hold among beliefs whether the believer recognizes them or not.

THE WEB OF BELIEF

Often in assessing beliefs we do best to assess several in combination. A very accomplished mechanic might be able to tell something about an automobile's engine by examining its parts one by one, each in complete isolation from the others, but it would surely serve his purpose better to see the engine as a whole with all the parts functioning together. So with what we believe. It is in the light of the full body of our beliefs that candidates gain acceptance or rejection; any independent merits of a candidate tend to be less decisive. To see why this should be, recall the characteristic occasion for questioning beliefs. It was the situation where a new belief, up for adoption, conflicts somehow with the present body of beliefs as a body. Now when a set of beliefs is incompatible together, we have a choice: we can restore consistency by rejecting any one of several of the beliefs. And it is not always easy to decide which one had better go.

Let Abbott, Babbitt, and Cabot be suspects in a murder case. No one else, let us suppose, would have stood to benefit from the victim's death, unless through burglary—and burglary can be excluded, since none of the victim's effects was disturbed. But Abbott has an alibi, in the register of a respectable hotel in Albany. Babbitt also has an alibi, for his brother-in-law testified that Babbitt was visiting him in Brooklyn at the time. Cabot pleads alibi too, claiming to have been watching a ski meet in the Catskills; but we have only his word for that. So we believe Abbott and Babbitt innocent and Cabot guilty.

But a little later Cabot documents his alibi—he had the good luck to have been caught by television in the sidelines at the ski meet. A new belief—that Cabot is innocent—is thus thrust upon us. Now we are forced to look back to our old set of beliefs and choose some, not all, of them for rejection. One of our old beliefs —that Cabot was guilty—has now certainly lapsed, but one or more others must go too.

For, our previous belief in Cabot's guilt had been supported by a combination of other beliefs. Insofar, our new belief in Cabot's innocence conflicts with that combination. The combination of beliefs comprised, we could say, these three: that Abbott did not commit the murder, that Babbitt did not, and that Abbott or Babbitt or Cabot did. Some one of these three beliefs must be rejected now that we believe Cabot not guilty, and one is enough to reject in order to restore consistency. So we look for the shakiest. Our belief that Babbitt did not commit the murder may be the belief to drop, since it rested only on the testimony of a sympathetic party, Babbitt's brother-in-law. Abbott's alibi was better, sustained as it was by a good hotel. Or again we might drop the third belief—that one of these three men committed the murder. This belief had its support in two anterior beliefs; one was that none but these three men had stood to gain from the death unless by burglary, and the other was that there had been no attempt at burglary. But it is doubtful that none but the three men had stood to gain from the death unless by burglary. A fourth man might well have stood to gain by serving, for a fee, as trigger man for Abbott or Babbitt or Cabot.

This illustrates the effort to decide which belief to reject, in a case of conflict, by comparing the individual evidence for the several beliefs. Between the two beliefs which at the end seem easiest to reject, in this example, we may or may not reach a decision, with or without help of some still further evidence.

Note a certain organization that helped to schematize the reasoning. From a mass of variously interlocking and conflicting beliefs, we somewhat arbitrarily separated out four for prominent placing, and then subordinated the others by calling them evidence for these four. The four beliefs chosen for prominence were:

> (1) that Abbott did not commit the crime,
> (2) that Babbitt did not,
> (3) that Abbott or Babbitt or Cabot did,

and, as lately discovered,

> (4) that Cabot did not.

These four already show contradiction. Then other relevant beliefs were sorted out under these, as evidence. We named six:

> (5) that only Abbott, Babbitt, and Cabot stood to gain from the murder apart from burglary,
> (6) that there was no burglary,
> (7) that Abbott is registered at an Albany hotel under the date of the murder,
> (8) that the hotel is reliable,
> (9) that Babbitt was at his brother-in-law's in Brooklyn at the time, and
> (10) that Cabot was televised in the Catskills at the time.

Finally, we resolved our contradiction by dropping belief (2), or perhaps (3), because of the comparative weakness of the subsidiary belief (9) or (5) as the case may be.

This organization was artificially imposed. We could instead have confronted all the beliefs (1) through (10) on an equal footing, appreciated that they were in contradiction, and finally decided to weed out (2) and (9), or perhaps (3) and (5). But the organization lightened our task: it focused our attention on four prominent beliefs among which to drop one, and then it sorted the six subsidiary beliefs under those four as mere aids to choosing which of the four to drop.

The strategy illustrated would seem in general to be a good one: divide and conquer. When a set of beliefs has accumulated to the point of contradiction, for instance the set (1) through (10) above, find the smallest selection of them you can that still involves contradiction; for instance (1) through (4). For we can be sure that we are going to have to drop one of the beliefs in that subset, whatever else we do. In reviewing and comparing the evidence for the beliefs in the subset, then, we will find ourselves carried back in a rather systematic way to other beliefs of the set. Eventually, perhaps we find ourselves dropping some of those other beliefs too; thus we drop (9) along with (2), or (5) with (3).

In probing the evidence, where do we stop? In probing the evidence for (1) through (4) we dredged up (5) through (10); but we could have probed further, for evidence for (5) through (10) in turn. In fact we did cite evidence in turn for (6) and for (9), as follows:

(11) that the victim's effects were not disturbed, and
(12) that Babbitt's brother-in-law said so.

In practice, the probing stops when we are satisfied how best to restore consistency: which ones to discard among the beliefs we have canvassed.

Our adjustment of a given inconsistent set of beliefs may be either decisive or indecisive, in the following sense. If it is decisive, each belief of the set is either kept or switched to disbelief. If it is indecisive, some of the beliefs simply give way to nonbelief; judgment on them is suspended. Where the inconsistent set of beliefs is (1) through (10) above, or indeed we may now say (1) through (12), one possible decisive adjustment that we considered consists in changing beliefs (2) and (9) to disbelief, and so accusing Babbitt. Another possible decisive adjustment that we considered consists in changing beliefs (3) and (5) to disbelief. This exonerates all three suspects of the physical act of murder, but leaves each of them under suspicion as possible instigator of the murder. If we cannot make up our minds between these two decisive adjustments, we may simply withdraw some of our beliefs—(2) and (3) anyway —in favor of nonbelief. Beliefs (5) and (9) might go over either into disbelief or into nonbelief; either way we settle for an indecisive adjustment, leaving a smaller set of beliefs. Such a course leaves it undecided whether Babbitt did the killing or someone other than Abbott, Babbitt, and Cabot did, with or without the connivance of any of these three. It leaves us ignorant, but consistent. Whether to leave matters thus will depend on what hopes we entertain of improving them, and how deeply we care to solve the crime.

If we do propose to persevere, there are two things we can do. We can look for clues in hopes of supplementing our poor stock of relevant beliefs. We can also go on probing the evidence for beliefs already entertained, particularly those lately suspended, to see if at some point we can promote nonbelief to belief or disbelief, or convert disbelief to belief, or vice versa.

EXERCISES

1. The remark "I wonder if John saw what was in the package?" may be imagined to have called forth from ten people the following ten replies:

I know he did.	I believe so.
I just know he did.	I don't believe so.
I don't know.	I believe not.
I know he didn't.	He must have.
He may have.	He can't have.

    Which of the ten people seem surest that John saw what was in the package? Which ones seem surest that John did not? How would you rank the remaining ones? Discuss.

2. Compose another micro-mystery, in the style of the one about Abbott, Babbitt, and Cabot, in which some early suspicion needs revising in the light of fresh evidence. Spell out your reasoning about the need for this revision, and indicate what alternative revisions are available.

3. Describe some situations in which you have found it necessary to revise some of your beliefs. Try to include some cases where the beliefs needing revision were deeply seated.

Chapter II

Observation

The structure seen in our murder mystery is seen also in the predictions and the checking operations that are so common in science and in everyday thinking. When our system of beliefs supports our expectation of some event and that event does not occur, we have the problem of selecting certain of our interlocking beliefs for revision. This is what happens when an experiment is made to check a scientific theory and the result is not what the theory predicted. The scientist then has to revise his theory somehow; he must drop some one or another, at least, of the beliefs which together implied the false prediction. This is also what happens, less formally, whenever something expected fails to happen; we are called upon to go back and revise one or another of the beliefs which, taken together, had engendered the false expectation.

The pattern is simply that, again, of the foregoing murder mystery. For our false expectation was a belief, like our false suspicion of Cabot; and the disbelief which has superseded it creates an inconsistency in the system. Toward settling just which beliefs to give up, we consider what beliefs had mainly underlain the false prediction, and what further beliefs had underlain these, and so on, as in the murder case. We stop such probing of evidence, as was remarked, when we are satisfied. But, failing satisfaction, is there no bottom where we are bound to stop? There is a bottom, not rock bottom perhaps, but bottom enough on the whole: the reports of observation.

Observations are the bottom. Or, in a figure that is in some ways more instructive, they are the boundary conditions. Imagine a taut elastic sheet, or drumhead, to which we have access only around the edges. We measure the tension at numerous points around the edges; here are the boundary conditions, the observations. From these data we arrive, by computation and speculation, at a theoretical quantity for the tension at each point in the interior of the sheet. For another illustration, imagine a computing machine in the form of a sealed black box. We observe the behavior of the machine by correlating input and output— the boundary conditions. From these data we arrive, speculatively, at a theory as to the internal structure of the machine. Observations—literally in these examples, figuratively in others —are the boundary conditions of a system of beliefs. By showing a prediction to have been wrong, observation demands the overhaul of a system of beliefs. At the same time, observation continues to underlie the system in its firmer portions.

When an observation shows that a system of beliefs must be overhauled, it leaves us to choose which of those interlocking beliefs to revise; this important fact has come up repeatedly. The beliefs face the tribunal of observation not singly but in a body. But note now that the observation sentence itself, the sentence that reports or predicts a present or imminent observation, is peculiar on this score. It does face the tribunal singly, in the usual case, and simply stands or falls with the observation that it reports or predicts. And, standing or falling, it sustains or lets down the system of beliefs that implied it.

The important difference between reports of observation and other sentences is best appreciated by reflecting on how we learn language. Some terms, and short sentences containing them, are learned in the sensible presence of something that the term describes, or in the circumstances that the sentence reports. This way of learning expressions is what philosophers call "ostensive." It is a simple matter of learning to associate the heard words with things simultaneously observed—a matter, as modern psychologists put it, of conditioning. Thus, we may venture to volunteer or assent to the word "yellow" in the presence of something yellow, on hearing others do so. This way of

13

responding will be reinforced, as psychologists say, by social approval or successful communication, and so become habitual. The part of language that we learn first must be learned ostensively, thus not depending on other language-learning.

Further vocabulary is acquired afterward by processes that depend on prior acquisitions. The simplest form that such derivative acquisition can take, though not the most frequent, is definition. The simplest form of definition, in turn, is that in which the new expression is equated outright to some expression that is presumed to have been already intelligible. Thus, if we suppose the words "parent," "brother," "married," and "man" already to have been somehow acquired, we might explain "uncle" and "bachelor" by equating them to "parent's brother" and "unmarried man." Other definitions are contextual; in these the new expression is not equated to anything outright, but systematic instructions are given for translating all desired sentences containing the expression. For instance, we might define "brother," not by formulating any direct substitute for the word by itself, but by systematically explaining all sentences in which the word occurs followed by "of." This we could do by translating "brother of x" as "male other than x whose parents are the parents of x." Or again we might define the connective "if and only if," not outright, but by systematically explaining all the compound sentences that are obtained by putting "if and only if" between sentences. We simply explain "p if and only if q" as "if p then q and if q then p."

But definition of either sort accounts for only a small fraction of our language learning, and even ostension itself accounts for only a modest part. A major source is an elaborate and largely unconscious process of abstraction and generalization from observed use. We guess the force of one sentence by noting its use in relation to other sentences; we grasp the use of a word by abstraction from sentences in which it turns up; and we learn how to build new sentences by copying the structure observed in old ones. There is much that could be said, and much more still to be learned, about these methods. But at any rate they are, like the more transparent method of definition, methods of derivative acquisition of language—they depend on prior acquisitions. Learning by ostension depends on no prior acquisitions. By ostension we learn to use and react to observation sentences.

Typical observation sentences are about bodies: "This is a

table," "This table is square," "The cat is on the mat." Always the situation that makes an observation sentence true will be a situation that is present when and where the sentence is truly uttered. Always, moreover, it will be intersubjectively observable; that is, it will be the sort of situation to which multiple witnesses could, if present, attest. Further, it will be a situation that the witnesses can witness one another's witnessing of. These three crucial traits are assured by the distinctive nature of ostension. The learner of the language has to be able to observe the relevant situation at the same time that he hears the veteran speaker affirm the sentence, and he has also to be able to observe that the speaker's affirming of the sentence is accompanied by his observing that same situation. Correspondingly, the veteran speaker who ventures to judge the learner's performance has to be able to observe that the learner, when he affirms the sentence, is observing the appropriate situation.

Some readers may care to pause here for a brief philosophical interlude. For there are two traits of observation sentences which, when considered side by side, invite a philosophical question. The distinguishing feature of observation sentences is that their whole occasion is the observable present occasion. Yet, as remarked, these sentences are commonly about enduring bodies— cats, mats, tables. How is this possible? That there are enduring bodies at all, behind the passing show of sensory appearance, is a point of physical theory—a rudimentary point, but still something beyond the observable present occasion. How then can a sentence about bodies be at the same time an observation sentence, for which the whole occasion for affirmation is the observable present?

This puzzle comes of viewing the matter from the wrong end. The special virtue of observation sentences is that we can in principle learn them by ostension as wholes, keyed as wholes to the appropriate observable occasions, before ever learning to link the component words to enduring bodies. "The cat is on the mat" can be learned ostensively as a unitary string of syllables in association with a certain range of possible scenes. All of us necessarily learned some observation sentences thus. Then, as we gradually caught on to the theory of enduring bodies, we came to attribute corporeal reference to component words. Learning by ostension, as a trained animal might, to associate whole observation sentences with appropriate patterns of stimulation, is a first indispensable step toward learning physical theory. We get on into the theory afterward, bit by bit, as we learn to dis-member the observation sentences and make further use of their component words. It is to this primary, ostensive learning of observation sentences as wholes that physical theory itself owes its vital continuing connection with sensory evidence.

Probably none of us in fact learned "The cat is on the mat" outright by ostension, but we could have. A likelier example is "(This is a) ball," or "Yellow," or "Mamma." An important trait of language is that people learn it by different routes and no record of the route is preserved in the words learned. What makes a sentence an observation sentence is not that it *was* learned ostensively but that it is of a sort that *could* have been. And what sort is that? We already said: it is a sentence whose whole occasion of affirmation, nearly enough, is the intersubjectively observable present occasion. This is a straightforward trait at-taching to some sentences and not others. And it is a trait that is socially traceable, for what it comes to is just that all speakers of the language, nearly enough, will assent to the sentence under the same concurrent stimulations. "The table is square" and "The cat is on the mat" will pass this test and so qualify as observation sentences. "This is a bachelor" will not qualify as an observation sentence, since one of two tested speakers may happen to know that the man pointed to is a bachelor while the other does not. We have, thus, a convenient social criterion for distinguishing between observation sentences and others. Namely, speakers of the language will ordinarily agree as to the truth or falsity of an observation sentence when they are stimulated alike.

We spoke of observation as the boundary condition. For some-one who is checking back over his beliefs after a prediction has gone wrong, his underlying observations are, we remarked, near rock bottom. The same is true for someone who is marshaling his evidence for a belief that has been challenged by a colleague. And it is here that the social trait just now attributed to obser-vation sentences is crucial—that all speakers assent to such a sentence under the same stimulations. As dissident theorists con-verge toward observation sentences they converge to agreement.

Are observation sentences then infallible? Nearly, if we set aside those offered disingenuously and those uttered by speakers who have not quite learned the language. Observation sentences, after all, are the sentences for which the evidence is present whenever the sentences are truly affirmed. It would strain the very meaning of the words, in such sentences, to suppose any appreciable fallibility; for the words are themselves acquired through the association of observation sentences with the observable circumstances of their utterance.

A trace of fallibility, indeed, there is. Normally, observation is the tug that tows the ship of theory; but in an extreme case the theory pulls so hard that observation yields. It can happen that a theory has long gone unchallenged, neatly conforming to countless relevant observations on every hand, and that now one observation conflicts with it. Chances are that we will waive the one wayward observation, attributing it to unexplained interference, even to hallucination. Moreover, if such alleged cases of hallucination tend to cluster in a few persons, who may then be seen as prone to hallucination, so much the better for our scientific conscience. There is then hope of accommodating the very waywardness of those wayward observations in a theory too, a theory of psychopathology. Law may thus be sought in the apparent breaches of law.

Even when observations persist in conflicting with a theory, the theory will not necessarily be abandoned forthwith. It will linger until a plausible substitute is found; the conflicting observations will stand unexplained, and the sense of crisis will mount.

> Galileo's contributions to the study of motion depended closely upon difficulties discovered in Aristotle's theory by scholastic critics. Newton's new theory of light and color originated in the discovery that none of the existing . . . theories would account for the length of the spectrum, and the wave theory that replaced Newton's was announced in the midst of growing concern about anomalies in the relation of diffraction and polarization effects to Newton's theory. Thermodynamics was born from the collision of two existing nineteenth-century physical theories, and quantum mechanics from a variety of difficulties surrounding black-body radiation, specific heats, and the photoelectric effect. Furthermore, in all these cases except that of Newton the awareness of anomaly had lasted so long and penetrated so deep that one can appropriately describe the fields affected by it as in a state of growing crisis. Because it demands . . . major shifts in the problems and techniques of normal science, the emergence of new theories is generally preceded by a period of pronounced professional insecurity. As one might expect, that insecurity is generated by the persistent failure of the puzzles of normal science to come out as they should. Failure of existing rules is the prelude to a search for new ones.[1]

[1] T. S. Kuhn, *The Structure of Scientific Revolutions* (Chicago and London: The University of Chicago, 1962) pp. 67f.

There are some points at which, without deliberate consideration of theories, all of us find it second nature to edit observation. We learn to take it that sticks appearing bent while partially immersed in water should in fact be judged straight. We learn not to suppose that the moon is larger when near the horizon than when higher in the sky. When the colors before us begin to vibrate, we do not imagine that the properties of light have changed. But in all these examples, again, we are at pains in the end to accommodate the waywardness of the observations in a theory too. The illusion of the immersed sticks is covered by a physical theory of refraction; the illusion of the low moon is coped with by some psychological hypotheses; and a general visual disruption is apt to set us speculating about something we ate or drank. Observations thus stubbornly retain their primacy. They remain the boundary conditions of our body of beliefs.

It must be confessed however that not all observations, or reports of observations, are so conscientiously accommodated. Some of them, uncongenial to existing theory, get passed over with even less acknowledgment than it would take to rate them as hallucinations. Persistent reports of occult experiences receive this short treatment, as also, of late, many of the reports of unidentified flying objects. Note, however, that a good scientist does not treat an uncongenial observation in this high-handed way when the observation is induced by an experiment of his own. For his experiment will have been designed for the very purpose of deciding between two alternative moves in the development of his theory, two preconceived alternative beliefs. But he will perhaps dismiss a puzzling observation, reported to him with palpable sincerity or even made by himself, if he has in mind no specific change of theory that might accommodate the observation and still jibe with previous data. Up to a point this high-handedness is justifiable. If a scientist were to interrupt existing projects in order to find a plausible hypothesis for every puzzling experience outside the laboratory, and if he were to lend a patient and judicious ear to every crank and gossip, he would learn less.

Scientists are so good nowadays at discovering truth that it is trivial to condone their methods and absurd to criticize them. At the same time it is evident that waiving observations is always a delicate business. A theory that is sustained only at the cost of systematic waiving is an undependable instrument of prediction and not a good example of scientific method.

Just because it is not feasible to accommodate all observations all the time, some philosophers have wanted to scout the whole idea of observation. Their doubts have been aggravated by a further consideration: the air of subjectivity that seems to them to render the very idea of observation hopelessly vague. Where the untrained eye observes a wired metal box, the trained eye observes a condenser. Where the untrained eye observes nothing, the trained eye observes the recent trace of a deer. But again these discrepancies are no ground for misgivings when properly viewed; they are only a play on the careless use of a word.

For philosophical purposes the notion of observation, and of observation sentence, needs to be taken with an unimaginative literalness. A straightforward criterion to the purpose was already noticed some three pages back: that all members of the community that concerns us are disposed, if asked, to assent to the sentence under the same stimulations of their sensory surfaces. Thus, suppose we were to ask each successive member of the community for a "yes" or "no" to the sentence in question, at the same time that we subject him to each of various stimulations. What makes the sentence count as an observation sentence, then, is that all members of the community, nearly enough, will say "Yes" to it under the same stimulations, and all will say "No" to it under the same stimulations. What counts as an observation sentence will be relative to the community chosen, but this is as it should be; "Deer track" and "Condenser" will qualify as observation sentences for communities of experts and not for wider communities. What meet the test of observationality for wider communities are sentences that more numerous speakers have learned to associate with concurrent stimulations—sentences like "Bent grass," "Wired box," and "The cat is on the mat." The discrepancies that clouded the notion of observationality came of not keeping track of what speech community was concerned. When we do keep track, observation takes its proverbial place as arbiter of science. Observation sentences for the arbitrating community are the sentences on which that community can reach immediate agreement under appropriate stimulation.

Commonly an observation sentence will cease to be an observation sentence when we change only the tense of its verb. For the remembrance of a past observation is not itself an observation. We can easily be mistaken now about an event that would have been all but unmistakable when it occurred, if it did occur. It is good scientific practice to guard against the fallibility of memory by making written records of important observations as they come. Practically speaking, such records of observation do indeed serve as present and enduring observation reports of events long past. Strictly and philosophically speaking, the records are themselves the objects of our new current observation. Our present observation of the records gives us indirect evidence of the past events recorded there, thanks to our knowledge of the forces and mechanisms that would have gone into producing the records. A preserved photograph of an event would be indirect evidence in the same way. Nor does either sort of record differ in essential respects from the deer track, as indirect evidence of an earlier passing of a deer.

Before concluding our discussion of observation sentences, it should be noted that in some philosophical writings this title is reserved for sentences very different from observation sentences as we have defined them. It is reserved for introspective reports like "I am in pain" and "I seem to see blue now." Such reports also have been rated as infallible. It must be conceded that they tend to be incontestable, because of the speaker's privileged access to his private experience. But on this very point they differ diametrically from observation sentences in our sense. The situations that make them true are not ones to which multiple witnesses could attest. What is open to public observation in such a case is rather the introspective report itself. What is comparable to the cat's being on the mat is not the man's feeling pain or seeing blue, but his reporting pain or blue—his verbal behavior. This verbal behavior is indeed available as a datum for further theorizing; it is a datum to which multiple witnesses might attest.

EXERCISES

1. Give as varied a list as you can of observation sentences. Are reports of unidentified flying objects observation sentences? Discuss.

2. Suppose that someone does not understand "midway," but that he does understand "twice as far," as in the context "x is twice as far from y as z is from w." Provide for him, on this basis, a contextual definition of "midway between."

3. Invent examples illustrating how one might use the process of abstraction to learn the use of the words "virtue," "know," and "normal."

4. Extend the list of examples in which we "find it second nature to edit observation."

Chapter III

Self-Evidence

We noted an important class of beliefs that do not rest on other beliefs. Those were the beliefs expressed by observation sentences. Now there is also another class of beliefs of which the same can be said: beliefs that are *self-evident*. What distinguishes these beliefs is that they look for support neither to other beliefs nor to observation. To understand them is to believe them.

Such a belief, when simple, is naturally too trivial to be worth stating (unless in books like this); for normally only news, in some sense, is worth stating. What are called "logical truths" are the readiest examples: "Every horse that is white is a horse." This particular truth illustrates a general logical principle: "Every *A* that is *B* is an *A*." Our instance comes from the general principle by substitution: "horse" for "*A*" and "white" for "*B*." As support of the particular case, however, the general principle is superfluous; for it cannot be more obviously true than its instance, which affirms so much less. Anyway, to adduce support to "Every horse that is white is a horse" would be to adduce coals to Newcastle.

To what do such truths owe their truth? Some philosophers claim that logical truths are true because of the meanings of the basic little logical words—in this case "every," "that," "is," and "an." Certainly we can defend their doctrine this far: if anyone were seriously to deny a sentence of the form "Every A that is B is an A," he would doubtless be giving odd meanings to those words. But this defense is more apparent than real. If on a cold day a man seriously remarks how warm it is, we have good reason to suppose he misunderstands a word. Perhaps he has associated "cold" with his native *caldo*, and hence "warm" with *freddo*. Yet it does not follow that "It is cold" is true simply because of the meanings of its words and independently of the weather. The simple fact is that whenever anyone denies a sentence which, in the circumstances or in general, is obviously true, we have evidence that he has missed a meaning. In particular, then, nothing has really been said to show that logical truth is *due* to meaning—nothing beyond calling logical truths self-evident, which is where we came in.

All truths depend on meanings at least in part, of course; for, by supplanting a word by some other that differs in meaning, we can make any true sentence false. Of a sentence that is obviously true and depends in no obvious way on observations or prior beliefs, one might then say that its truth is based solely on meanings—just because there is no other basis to point to. If this is the doctrine, well and good—so long as we do not take it to be telling us anything.

Self-evidence, whatever its cause, is the conspicuous trait of "Every horse that is white is a horse." It cannot be said to be a trait of all logical truths, but there is a derivative trait that can. When a logical truth is too complicated to be appreciated out of hand, it can be proved from self-evident truths by a series of steps each of which is itself self-evident—in a word, it can be *deduced* from them. This trait is *demonstrability*. It may be called *absolute* demonstrability when there is need to distinguish it from the *relative* case where something is deducible only from some previously established or accepted beliefs or stated hypotheses which are not themselves self-evident.

The trait of self-evidence is not hard and fast. Some truths may be self-evident for one person and in need of proof for another person. An example, perhaps, is the logical truth:

If you help none who help themselves, you do not help yourself.

If we have a friend who does not find the truth of this sentence self-evident, we might try to prove the sentence to him by deriving it from one or more sentences that are self-evident to him, by steps which are self-evident to him. For instance, giving our friend no great credit, we might start with the self-evident truth:

> In helping yourself, you help at least one self-helper (namely yourself).

From this it self-evidently follows that

> If you do not help at least one self-helper, you do not help yourself

and thence that

> If you help none who help themselves, you do not help yourself,

which was to be proved.

We see from this example how even a brief logical truth may fail to be self-evident, but still be absolutely demonstrable. It is an important fact that absolutely demonstrable truths may fall so far short of being self-evident as to be extraordinarily difficult to see or even counter-intuitive. As we observe from the uses of computers, the linking of large numbers of trivial little steps may yield knowledge that is itself neither trivial nor obvious.

The logical truths are absolutely demonstrable. How much territory do they take in? A way of demarcating it is suggested by the schematism that we used in "Every A that is B is an A." Here is a formula built of what we may call logical particles— "every," "that," "is," and "an"—along with letters as blanks, substitution for which gives the formula's instances. This is a formula, or form, all of whose instances are true sentences, indeed logical truths. The suggestion is that in general we call a sentence logically true when it is an instance of some form built of just logical particles and blanks, and all instances of that form are true.

The form may be called a *logical form*, meaning that besides blanks it contains just logical particles. Further, it may be called *valid*, meaning that all its instances are true. So the suggestion is that we call a sentence *logically true* when it is an instance of a valid logical form. Thus "Every horse that is white is a horse" counts as logically true because it is an instance of the valid logical form "Every A that is B is an A."

Our other example was, in effect, "Whoever helps none who help themselves does not help himself." It is an instance of the valid logical form "Whoever Rs none who R themselves does not

R himself." Here "R" is a blank for a transitive verb like "help" and the other words are again, nearly enough, logical particles.[1]

Care must be taken not to abuse the logical forms. "Every A that is B is an A" may be all very well, but its variant "Every BA is an A," as in "Every white horse is a horse," skirts pitfalls. What are we to say of "Every expectant mother is a mother," or "Every intellectual dwarf is a dwarf"? In view of such examples, the foregoing definition of logical truth in terms of logical forms must be seen as only a first step. For its fuller application we would need to consider systematically how to construe various of our idioms. We would need to develop techniques by which we could paraphrase given discourse into sentences that make plain what logical forms that discourse might reasonably be taken to be exhibiting. Natural languages being as they are, logical relationships are not always laid bare by syntax alone. These matters of paraphrase, or of regimentation, fall largely within the province of symbolic logic and its application.

We have before us a definition, if only provisional, of what it is to be logically true: it is to be an instance of a valid logical form. This definition depends on the prior definition of validity, which used a prior general notion of truth; and it depends on the prior definition of logical form, which used a prior notion of logical particle. Observe that there is in this definition of logical truth itself no guarantee that every logical truth is demonstrable. For every logical truth to be demonstrable, there have to be self-evident logical truths in sufficient abundance to enable deduction of every further logical truth. But this requirement does in fact turn out to be fulfilled; at any rate it does if in defining logical truth we are not too generous with the category of logical particles. For note that we have thus far merely availed ourselves of a dozen logical particles, as needed, and said nothing of their further extent.

Prominent also among the logical particles are "if," "or," "and," "but," and "some." Actually these and others can by a vigorous

---

[1] Or, if we prefer to be more pedantic about logical particles, we might say rather that "whoever" and "who" and "him" are not pure logical particles, because they involve the notion of person, which belongs rather to anthropology than to logic. Then we would paraphrase "whoever" in our example as "whatever person," and "none" as "no person," and "who" as "which," and "himself" as "itself," and thus isolate the valid logical form "Whatever A Rs no A which Rs itself does not R itself." Here "A" is a blank for any common noun such as "person," and "R" is a blank for any transitive verb such as "help," and the other words are incontestably logical particles.

paraphrasing of contexts be reduced to the small fund previously noted, and that fund can be reduced in turn. In some theoretical work in logic, such economies are useful. But no matter; what is more worth noting is that if we limit the category of logical particles essentially to the ones that we have used here, then all logical truths, so defined, are indeed demonstrable. This important fact was established only in 1928–30 by work of Skolem and Gödel.

We have pictured the proof of a logical truth as consisting in derivation from self-evident beginnings by self-evident steps. It should be mentioned that logical theory in its modern estate is more formal. Instead of just saying that the beginnings are to be self-evident, the logician specifies some valid logical forms as his explicit starting point. These he calls axioms. Likewise, instead of just leaving any further valid logical forms to be derived from the axioms by self-evident steps, he specifies certain allowable steps, or *rules of inference*. For instance, he might start with axioms including, among a half dozen others, the valid logical form "p or not p" (using "p" to stand for sentences). One of his rules of inference might be this: from "p or q" infer "q or p." Applying this rule to the axiom "p or not p," he gets as a theorem the new valid logical form "not p or p." From this in turn, by some other of his rules, he gets a second theorem. From a small but judicious choice of axioms and rules of inference (less trivial on the average than the present examples), every valid logical form can be generated as a theorem. This is a somewhat better statement of the completeness theorem just now attributed to Skolem and Gödel.

Complete coverage of logical truth can be managed equally by each of many formal proof procedures, in particular by each of many alternative sets of axioms and rules of inference. Formal proof procedures are also available which follow other patterns than that of axioms and rules of inference. We will not elaborate on the various alternatives here; let us just say what all formal proof procedures have in common. The keynote is susceptibility to routine check by inspection of formulas. We can tell on inspection whether a proposed sentence falls under one of the axioms, and we can tell on inspection whether a proposed step falls under one of the rules of inference. If a proof procedure departs from the axiom and rule pattern, still its applications must be similarly susceptible to check. Otherwise we do not call it a proof procedure.

The development of formal proof procedures was necessary

for a deep understanding of logic—the kind of understanding reflected in the theorem of Skolem and Gödel, among others. That development must not, however, be allowed to obscure the part that is played, now as before, by self-evidence. However formal a proof procedure may be, the trustworthiness of the theorems that it generates still depends ultimately upon our conviction that each of the axioms is logically valid and our conviction that none of the rules of inference can lead from a form that is valid to a form that is not.

Absolute demonstrability is no monopoly of the logical truths, and neither is self-evidence. Thus, take "No bachelor is married," or "The parts of parts of a thing are parts of the thing," or "Every brother has a brother or sister." These do not meet the definition of logical truth; there are no appropriate logical forms we can cite. Still they have as much title to self-evidence as the logical truths. They have as much right to be said to be true by virtue of the meanings of words, too—and as little. We saw the problem of making sense of that attribution. At any rate these, like the logical truths, are self-evident. And like the self-evident logical truths they give rise, through steps of self-evident inference, to a teeming posterity of further truths which, though less evident, still qualify as absolutely demonstrable.

There are also propositions which, though their truth would never be questioned, seem not to deserve the title of self-evidence. An example is "There have been dogs." The title of self-evidence would seem odd here mainly because *other* evidence is so evident: our observations of dogs. This example is not on all fours with the logical truth about horses considered above; for observations of horses had nothing to do with that one. Thus, "self-evidence" connotes something besides certainty; it also has a negative force in that it excludes observation as irrelevant. Put the other way round, if observation is relevant to our acceptance of a claim then the claim fails to qualify as self-evident.

Logical truths, when brief, are so largely trivial that one may wonder what is important about the whole category. Its main importance accrues to it through the derivative notion of logical implication. This notion can be defined in terms of logical truth as follows: one sentence logically implies another when the compound sentence which we get by combining the two in the fashion "If p then q" is logically true. For instance, the sentence "The world was without form and void" logically implies the sentence "The world was void"; and to say that it does so is simply to attribute logical truth to the sentence "If the world was without form and void then the world was void." Or, to take a less trivial example, the sentence "Someone helps all who do not help themselves" logically implies the sentence "Someone helps himself"; and to say that it does so is simply to attribute logical truth to the sentence "If someone helps all who do not help themselves then someone helps himself." Logical implication is also called logical consequence or deducibility, but in reverse order. "Someone helps himself" is a logical consequence of, or logically deducible from, "Someone helps all who do not help themselves." Logical implication is the relation which relates any theory or hypothesis to its logical consequences.

The term "implication," and its alternatives "consequence" and "deducible," have also a broader and vaguer application without the qualifier "logical." One sentence is said to imply another whenever, starting with the one sentence plus perhaps some self-evident truths, you can get to the other sentence by a series of self-evident steps. This broad notion of implication or consequence or deducibility is useful and widely used, but vague insofar as we have not settled just what to count as self-evident. Logical implication is the well-defined core of implication, and the techniques governing it are the central business of logic.

There will be no need in these pages to draw a sharp line around self-evidence. We have recognized that there are self-evident truths, and that these include a sufficient nucleus of logical truths to generate the rest of the logical truths by self-evident steps. We have noted also that self-evident truths can be accounted for by meanings of words, but then again that such an account does not come to much.

Speaking of the demonstrability of the logical truths reminds us of mathematics, where proof is so much the pattern. May we not say of mathematical truths generally what we have said of logical truths, that all are demonstrable? This would mean that each truth of mathematics was either self-evident or derivable from self-evident truths by self-evident steps—and such was once the general belief. However, difficulties arise. They are best illustrated in the area known as set theory.

Sets, or classes, are basic for mathematics; many of the fundamental portions of mathematics seem to require the notion of set for their systematic development. In fact many a reasonable philosopher of mathematics contends that mathematics is exclusively about sets. Sets, as we understand them here, are objects determined by their members, that is, by the objects that belong to them. So to specify just which members a set has is to specify the set. Now specification of members need not proceed by a simple listing of them; obviously such listing cannot be achieved for sets with infinitely many members. So we often specify a set's membership, and therewith the set itself, by citing some condition that is both necessary and sufficient for membership in that set. Thus, we might specify the set of even integers by citing the condition of being the double of an integer; this condition is met by all and only the members of the set. It is natural to suppose that whenever we give such a condition we succeed in specifying a set—the set whose members are exactly the objects that meet the condition. Once accustomed to speaking of sets in this way, one might indeed suppose it self-evident that there is a set for each condition citable. Brilliant mathematicians did once suppose this. Yet it cannot be true.

For consider the condition of *not* being a set that is a member of itself. This is the condition, in short, of non-self-membership. Almost any object that comes to mind fulfills this condition; for example, the set of even integers, not being itself the double of an integer, surely does so. But there is nonetheless no set whose members are exactly the objects meeting the condition of non-self-membership. For suppose there were a set of just those objects. Let us call the alleged set x. Just the things that are not members of themselves are members of x. But then, in particular, x is a member of x just in case x is not a member of itself. We are caught in contradiction. We have to conclude that there is no such set x after all. *Nothing has as members all and only what do not have themselves as members.* This is even a logical truth. Its logical form, "Nothing Rs all and only what does not R itself," is a valid logical form.

The sentence italicized above illustrates that even a fairly brief logical truth can be not merely unobvious but, indeed, counter-intuitive. Named for its discoverer, it is known as Russell's paradox. It is the simplest of the many paradoxes of set theory. It is a paradox of set theory though a logical truth. What is paradoxical about it is that it runs against a set-theoretic expectation—the expectation that there be a set for each expressible membership condition.

One lesson of these paradoxes is that self-evidence is not to be attributed lightly. Another is that the truths of set theory, or the sentences of set theory that are to be regarded as truths, cannot be expected to be absolutely demonstrable (as logical truths were); that is, not derivable from self-evident truths by self-evident steps. What one now does in set theory is adopt special axioms of set existence, not as self-evident truths but as hypotheses comparable to the hypotheses of theoretical physics. One then deduces consequences, by steps of inference which are themselves of course still self-evident. One examines the consequences and then perhaps tinkers with the axioms some more, much as one might with hypotheses in physics, to see if a neater system can be devised to the same practical purposes.

Another principle long taken by mathematicians to be self-evident was the Euclidean parallels postulate, which asserts that there is exactly one parallel to a given line through any point off that line. The parallels postulate has been shown not to be deducible from the other Euclidean postulates. On the contrary, it is replaceable by any of various contrary postulates without loss of systematic consistency. And far from being requisite for our physics, the parallels postulate has even been supplanted there by one of those variants.

Not all mathematics has lost touch with self-evidence to this degree. A much better behaved part is elementary number theory, which is roughly the arithmetic and algebra of the positive integers. Here there are no known paradoxes—no propositions that seem self-evident and prove false. Better behaved though it be, however, elementary number theory presents some easily formulable questions that have resisted definitive answer for centuries.

Here there is a situation very unlike what one finds in the logical truths. Gödel has shown that no formal proof procedure for elementary number theory can be complete. No proof procedure can be so strong that all the truths of elementary number theory (and no falsehoods) admit of proof under it. Every proof procedure must miss some truths of elementary number theory or let in some falsehoods. In the light of Gödel's result it is quite implausible that all truths of elementary number theory are, like the logical truths, absolutely demonstrable in our sense: derivable from self-evident truths by self-evident steps.

Thus, it seems that mathematics generally (including geometry and number theory as well as set theory) is from an evidential point of view more like physics and less like logic than was once supposed. On the whole the truths of mathematics can be deduced not from self-evident axioms, but only from hypotheses which, like those of natural science, are to be judged by the plausibility of their consequences.

Other kinds of claims have also been held self-evident. There are the claims vaguely known as *limiting principles*: principles, broadly philosophical in tone, that disallow one or another general sort of scientific hypothesis. One such is the principle that nothing can come out of nothing, better known by its venerable Latin equivalent *Ex nihilo nihil fit*. This purports to tell us not what there is in the universe, but that, whatever there is, each thing was either always there or sprang from something else.

Now what is remarkable about this principle is that it has lately had a narrow escape from repudiation, a curious indignity for an allegedly self-evident principle to have to suffer. For there has been in recent years a staunchly supported, if bizarre, cosmological theory called the *steady-state* theory. It holds that hydrogen atoms are continually coming into existence without coming from anything at all. This, the theory goes, is how we are to explain the observed density of the universe. We know empirically that each galaxy is rapidly receding from all others. If we assume what has been called the "perfect cosmological principle,"—that the major motions in the universe are roughly uniform through time as well as space—then, were there not "continuous creation," the density of the universe would by now be much less than it is found to be. Although the steady-state theory sounds implausible, it was defended by some reputable astronomers as the solution to a paradox.

The steady-state theory was put forward as a rival to another cosmological theory, which had taught rather that in the beginning there was a cosmic explosion whence the recession of the galaxies began. We can represent this rivalry as a conflict of two limiting principles; the steady-state theory sustains the perfect cosmological principle at the cost of sacrificing the *Ex nihilo nihil*, while the explosion theory does the opposite. It happens that the steady-state theory has after all been losing out to the explosion theory, because of discoveries about the age of galaxies. So we learn here that limiting principles are not in general self-evident, being capable of conflicting. And we learn also that principles with even one foot in physics are answerable to empirical findings.

Another limiting principle to view warily is "Every event has a cause." As a philosopher's maxim it may seem safe enough if the philosopher is willing to guide it around recalcitrant facts. But this principle, in the face of quantum theory, needs extensive guiding. For if present physics is correct, there are events that are subject only to statistical and not rigidly determinate laws. This limiting principle can, like any other, be retained if one is willing to make enough sacrifices for it. But insofar as it purports to be a principle of physics, it cannot be counted as self-evident even if it somehow survives modern quantum theory.

On the whole, then, the limiting principles measure up poorly to standards of self-evidence. Logic and mathematics seem to be the only domains where self-evidence manages to rise above triviality; and this it does, in those domains, by a linking of self-evidence on to self-evidence in the chain reaction known as proof. And even mathematics lends itself only partially to such treatment; this was brought home to us by Russell's paradox, Euclid's postulate of parallels, and Gödel's incompleteness theorem.

Self-evidence is sometimes ascribed to judgments of moral value. Instances of such ascription in the Declaration of Independence come to mind; but surely those commendable sentiments have been less universally shared, early and late, than self-evidence would require. A moral precept that perhaps has more of a claim to self-evidence is "One should not inflict needless pain." Mostly, however, what the ascription of self-evidence to a moral precept is apt to reflect is just a resolution that the precept is to be regarded as basic and hence as exempt from discussion. We resolve to treat such a maxim as a starting point rather than as standing in need of support itself. But even here, should several principles be advanced, questions of their consistency might very well arise. For add "One should not tell lies" to "One should not inflict needless pain"; these two mild injunctions can combine to create practical dilemmas in imaginable cases.

EXERCISES

1. Add to the list of pitfalls for "Every BA is an A." Hint: The animal kingdom is a rich source, as in "glass menagerie" and "sitting duck." Then find some second logical form which, like "Every BA is an A," appears valid but faces pitfalls of its own. List some of those pitfalls.

2. Add to the list of self-evident truths that are not logical truths, aiming for maximum variety among the truths listed. Then try to find some truths that seem neither clearly self-evident nor clearly not self-evident, and explain why you regard their status as doubtful.

3. Legend has it that there is a barber who shaves all and only those who do not shave themselves. Use a valid logical form to lay the legend to rest. How about a bibliography that lists exactly those bibliographies that fail to list themselves?

4. Find valid logical forms that testify to the logical truth of each of these:

    Whoever hurts himself hurts someone who hurts someone.

    Either everything eaten by a whale is eaten by a mammal or not every whale is a mammal.

5. By self-evident steps from a self-evident beginning, prove this:

    If God helps those who do not help themselves, God helps Himself.

Chapter IV

Testimony

Two basic ways in which language serves us are these: as a means of getting others to do what we want them to, and as a means of learning from others what we want to know. In the one way it affords us, vicariously, more hands to work with; in the other, more eyes to see with. It is to our interest to predict what will happen, and what would happen if we did one thing or another. Observation is a vital ingredient in all such prediction, and our chances of prediction are much increased by increased observation. So in its yield of vicarious observation, through the testimony of others, language confers a major benefit.

This testimonial or information-gathering function of language has as its primitive vehicle the observation sentence. This, we saw in Chapter II, is the part of language that everyone acquires or can acquire by ostension; in other words, by a direct conditioning of sentences to the relevant stimulations. So when we hear an observation sentence that reports something beyond our own experience, we gain evidence that the speaker has the stimulation appropriate for its utterance, even though that stimulation does not reach us. Such, in principle, is the mechanism of testimony as an extension of our senses. It was the first and greatest human device for stepping up the observational intake. Telescopes, microscopes, radar, and radio astronomy are later devices to the same end.

In speaking of enlarged or vicarious observation, we indulge, indeed, in a certain figure of speech. In Chapter II we talked of the recording of observations as affording present observation reports of events long past; and we reflected then that this was a figure of speech since, literally speaking, the record is the object of present observation and is only causally connected with observations long past. Similarly, in the case of the instruments, it is only the lens image or the microphotograph or the radar blip that is literally the object of observation. The object thereby revealed, the dark star or the protein molecule or whatever, is of course literally an unobserved object with which our observations are only causally connected. Similarly, in the case of another man's observation report, our observation in the literal sense is limited to the sound of his words—words with which *his* reported observations are causally connected. Especially in this last case, we in practice make the causal leap without a moment's reflection, because of the social nature of our very learning of the primitive vocabulary of observation. We learned this vocabulary in the first place by linking the sound of another's words to observations shared at the time of their utterance.

It is natural and often convenient to speak thus of enlarged or vicarious observation. But it is important also to reflect on the figurativeness of the usage, lest we forget that the observations figuratively so-called are far more fallible than the real thing. There are all the technical disorders that can interfere with telescopes, microscopes, and radar. There is also the fallibility of verbal testimony. Let us think a little about it.

Observation sentences, taken narrowly, are comparatively foolproof. That is what makes them the tribunal of science. It is when we move to other sentences that the danger of mistaken testimony soars. On the other hand neither the observation sentences nor the others are knaveproof. What about lies?

It would be a sorry world if we could not usually trust our fellow man. The great and ancient value of testimony as an extension of our senses would be gone. No one would like that. Therefore, it may appear, it behooves no one to lie. This reasoning, however, unfortunately for all of us, is erroneous. A melancholy truth of moral philosophy is involved here which applies not only to lying. The melancholy general point is that what a man gains from the law-abiding behavior of his fellows can be further augmented by his own violations. Take the case of a burning theater. A man's chance of escape is best if he bolts for the door and others file out in orderly fashion. His chances are poor if everyone bolts for the door. However, his own bolting will not itself cause others to bolt, not soon enough or in sufficient numbers to destroy his advantage. Similar remarks apply to all sorts of cheating. This is dangerous information, and the reader may take it as a compliment that we have ventured to share it with him. Anyway the fat was already in the fire. This is why society establishes legal penalties against theft and various other forms of cheating. The penalties offset the private advantage.

There is no general law against lying. Yet there is a marked tendency for people to tell the truth, as they see it, at least when the lie offers no conspicuous gain. It is as if an instinctive leaning toward truthfulness were gene-linked and had been favored by natural selection. Certainly a general tendency to truthfulness on the part of a society has great survival value, giving each of us, as remarked, more eyes to see with. Truthfulness is essential, in large part, to the survival value of language itself. Still, instead of looking for a veracity gene, perhaps we can account for this happy tendency in terms of the very mechanisms that make for the learning of language itself. Our learning of the primitive vocabulary of observation sentences consists, after all, in our learning to associate it with the appropriate sensory stimulations. Small wonder then if those same stimulations dispose us in future to affirm the properly associated observation sentences. Lying is an effortful deviation from the conditioned response. We have here made the point only for observation sentences, but something similar would seem to apply also to the obscurer and more complicated processes that go into the learning of higher parts of language.

If a force for veracity can thus be found in the very mechanism of language learning, a force for credulity can be found there equally. We learn to use expressions in the circumstances in which we find them used by others. In effect, therefore, we proceed on the implicit assumption that people were using the expressions fittingly and not in lies. It is an interesting question, even, how we ever attain to the temerity of viewing someone's statement as false. Why do we not always continue as learners of language and so accept each statement, together with its circumstances of utterance, as just that much further evidence of how the words are used? In answer to this philosophical question we might say that the turning point depends partly on how complex a language we will accept. Instead of construing special occurrences of certain words in special ways in order to count a man's statement true, we find it simpler after a point to count it false. In so doing we are apt to be guided also, however unconsciously, by hypotheses regarding plausible processes. By what processes, we may unconsciously ask ourselves, would that speaker himself ever have learned a language that was complicated in those ways? And by what more plausible processes might he have been caused to utter an intentional or inadvertent falsehood in this instance?

These reflections have given us cause to expect a built-in tendency toward veracity on the part of speakers and toward credulity on the part of listeners. Such tendencies are indeed the rule, and a harmonious pair of tendencies they are. However, it behooves us to watch the second tendency critically in ourselves. Veracity is generally admirable, if not always prudent; but credulity, in more than modest measure, is neither admirable nor prudent. In general, the way to keep our credulity within proper bounds is to continue to think, but consciously now, of plausible processes. It is on this score that observation sentences stand forth as fairly foolproof; whether to believe them hinges on questions of the speaker's morals and motives. But even the remembrance of a past observation, we noted, is not itself an observation; and the connection of most sentences with observation sentences is much more remote. Such remoteness brings with it all the opportunities for error with which we are so familiar. Thus, when assessing testimony other than pure observation reports we must keep this increasing danger in mind and take into consideration what opportunities the speaker may plausibly have had for gathering evidence for his claim. Such consideration of mechanism is needed, in these cases, in addition to questions of the speaker's morals and motives. Considerations of the one kind and the other give us reason to prefer the testimony of reference books to a neighbor's hearsay, and both to the claims of advertisers.

In courts of law the testimony of witnesses is customarily judged in part on how much of what they say appears to be favorable to them. It is easier to believe the man who tells us something he would appear to prefer concealed than the one whose testimony proclaims his own excellence or innocence. The assessing of courtroom testimony draws heavily on what one understands about human psychology and behavior under stress. The attorney who cross-examines must be able to sense what portions of the testimony might prove vulnerable. He must call together all that he believes about the case and the witness, all that he has learned about cross-examination from his own experience and study, then decide how to proceed. The courtroom is worthy of the attention of anyone who is inclined toward taking too much of what he is told at face value. It teaches a stern lesson. People disguise the truth in certain situations, whether out of deviousness, self-deception, ignorance, or fear. They also, of course, misremember, misjudge, and misreason.

It can be useful to form the habit of filing in one's memory, as it were, the sources of one's information. For it can happen that sources once trusted will lose their authority for us, and one would then like to know which beliefs might merit reassessment. We may come to mistrust a source on moral grounds, having found signs of private interests and corruption, and we may also come to mistrust a source on methodological grounds, having found signs of hasty thinking and poor access to data.

Say you believe that Millard Fillmore, the thirteenth President of the United States, was born on January 7, 1800. Why do you believe this? You might say that you remember hearing it in a lecture, or that you looked it up in an encyclopedia—or even that its inclusion as an example in this paragraph is your ground. But of the last you should be cautious. We might be giving an example of mistaken belief. In fact we are not; if you wish, you may now pause to verify that the cited date is correct.

Now did that convince you? If so, you trust us as authorities, at least on this. The invitation to look it up for yourself may have increased your confidence in the claim. Beware of such devices; a writer or speaker can expect not to be taken up on an invitation like this, so he gains by its apparent forthrightness while risking little. If a speaker ordered "Believe it because I tell you to," you might have answered his arrogance with skepticism. The point is that whether or not you accept the claim made by someone else depends on how much you trust him on the matter.

An author of this book remarked after walking about the principality of Monaco, "Just think—only eight square miles!" "I don't see how you even get eight out of it," his brother replied. The map was conclusive: you couldn't. Yet the Encyclopedia

Britannica, the World Almanac, Scott's stamp album, various American atlases, and the gazetteers in the dictionaries had agreed on eight square miles. Hachette and Larousse turned out to agree rather on 150 hectares, or less than three fifths of a square mile. A subsequent check of the Britannica (eleventh edition) revealed arresting detail: "Area about 8 sq. m., the length being 2¼ m. and the width varying from 165 to 1100 yds." Even this arithmetical absurdity had not prevented the producers of all those other reference books from copying the figure of eight square miles, if the Britannica was their source. We are happy to report that the myth is now broken and all recent "sources" consulted give, nearly enough, 0.59 square miles. But there is very likely some equally unwarranted figure on another topic that we are all accepting still, or even newly.

The policy of seeking safety in numbers by checking multiple sources is an excellent precaution; but, as the above example illustrates, it can fail when the sources are not independent. No one would check a newspaper report by checking more copies of the same newspaper. There is a saying that 4×10^7 Frenchmen can't be wrong, but the contrary is the case if they all believe what one wrong Frenchman tells them. In the foregoing example, admittedly, the Frenchmen were right.

For many claims, the typical endorsement is that they are "common knowledge." Common knowledge seems to consist of whatever is regarded by large numbers of persons to be true and by almost no one to be false. Preponderance of believers over disbelievers, rather than over nonbelievers, is what is in point, because it is nonbelief, not disbelief, that ignorance breeds. And on almost any subject there are many who have managed to remain ignorant. Now this question: Do we give sufficient backing to a claim if we note that it qualifies as "common knowledge," assuming that there is no question but that it does qualify?

What backing suffices depends on what it is to suffice for. In everyday exchanges we are inclined to accept without further issue what we take to be common knowledge. Indeed, we declare our acceptance in so describing it, since to speak of something as known is to speak of it as true. So the very use of the term tends to be question-begging—one reason why we were at pains to paraphrase it more neutrally above. Given, then, only that condition: believed by many and disbelieved by almost no one. What can we say?

First, it might be instructive to determine the composition of the segment of the population that holds the belief. It might also be helpful to know how they came to hold it, and whether it concerns matters on which we should expect them to be well-informed. But more important still is the question of the belief's source, and of how, if at all, it was first established. What kinds of evidence would have been appropriate for it and were such grounds available, in the first instance, for its support? For planethood of Neptune there was the investigation of astronomers; for depth of the Pacific the researches of oceanographers; for Hannibal's Alpine excursion the writings of his day and their verification by historians; for the Pythagorean theorem the deductions of mathematicians; for the superiority of one species of can opener over another the long and suffering experience of housewives. Some items of common knowledge, like the last two, we can verify afresh, needing only a little mathematics on the one hand and a few utensils on the other. Others not, though we can still consult authority. What stands open to fresh verification may merit special confidence, since such a belief has been withstanding greater risk of disproof. Thus, in the case of what we ourselves are in poor position to verify, continuing acceptance of it by those in better position might be our touchstone.

But as a touchstone it is fallible. The long and remarkable history of theories having the sun revolve about the earth may serve as a chastening reminder. If anything was ever taken to be common knowledge, the geocentric view certainly qualified in its time. And it had a long time, centuries over which it was repaired and repaired again but never discarded. Here the attitude of conservatism toward belief, on balance a helpful attitude, served to hinder. Nor can we dismiss this misbelief as one that was based on insufficient investigation; at the time it seemed well supported from both the experiential and philosophic poles. That a substance called the ether filled all space was basic to the physics of a hundred years ago; yet, this too came to be abandoned. And who doubts that it was once very generally supposed that air transportation for beings so badly equipped for it as humans was only to be had in flights of fancy?

The reason such widespread misbeliefs can thrive is that the ignorance of relevant truths is often accompanied by ignorance of that ignorance. So we must recognize that there are almost certain to be many items of today's so-called common knowledge, some springing directly from science and some not, that will illustrate the follies of our age in the next century's textbooks.

We like to believe that much of what we hold in common is firmly established and will stand as long as there are men to believe it. Probably we are justified in such confidence. But almost certainly too, if the intellectual history of our species be any guide at all, much of what we hold in common will come to be repudiated. The lesson is one not of despair, but of humility.

At least one famous writer held that in certain matters—he was actually talking about religion—one is called upon to believe things that the evidence mightily opposes.[1] He insisted that one's ability to do this was a test of one's faith; one proved one's faith by believing what was, normally speaking, unbelievable. Taken at its word this doctrine is preposterous. To persist in bucking the full weight of evidence is to persist in being unreasonable; and to extol the practice is even more wretched. Actually, we can recast the doctrine in a way that makes it less foolish. We often accept jarring beliefs when someone we greatly trust presents them; and such acceptance need not be seen as flying in the face of evidence, since part of the evidence available to us is whatever attests to the reliability of our informant. Acceptability turns, as always, on a weighing of the total evidence.

[1] The reader may recognize here the view of the Danish philosopher Kierkegaard or of his ancient predecessor Tertullian.

EXERCISES

1. Compile as varied a list as you can of sources of testimony on which you commonly rely. Possible examples: certain reference books, your physician, persons who give you telephone messages, the Weather Lady.

2. Recall some cases in which you found that you had been misinformed by sources you had thought reliable. Did these cases lead you to reappraise the reliability of those sources? If not, how did you account for the fact that you had been misinformed?

3. Find some nontrivial items of misinformation in reference books. If this proves too hard, try newspapers. It will suffice for you to find statements that contradict one another, though that alone will not establish which assertions are the mistaken ones.

Testimony

4. Compile as varied a list as you can of beliefs that you regard as common knowledge. Comment on your own reasons for accepting some of them. Then try to think of some beliefs that were once taken as common knowledge but are now rejected.

Chapter V

Hypothesis

Some philosophers once held that whatever was true could in principle be proved from self-evident beginnings by self-evident steps. The trait of absolute demonstrability, which we attributed to the truths of logic in a narrow sense and to rather little else, was believed by those philosophers to pervade all truth. They thought that but for our intellectual limitations we could find proofs for any truths, and so, in particular, predict the future to any desired extent. These philosophers were the rationalists. Other philosophers, a little less sanguine, had it that whatever was true could be proved by self-evident steps from two-fold beginnings: self-evident truths and observations. Philosophers of both schools, the rationalists and the somewhat less sanguine ones as well, strained toward their ideals by construing self-evidence every bit as broadly as they in conscience might, or somewhat more so.

Actually even the truths of elementary number theory are presumably not in general derivable, we noted, by self-evident steps from self-evident truths. Surely the further truths that are deducible by self-evident steps from self-evident truths *plus* observations must still comprise only a pretty slim portion of the truths of nature. In fact, they comprise only a slim portion of our eminently reasonable beliefs.

Hypothesis

It is now recognized that deduction from self-evident truths and observation is not the sole avenue to truth nor even to reasonable belief. A dominant further factor, in solid science as in daily life, is *hypothesis*. In a word, hypothesis is guesswork; but it can be enlightened guesswork. Newton saw hypotheses as something to disavow: "Hypotheses non fingo." But nowadays we appreciate that it is not the part of scientific rigor to disavow hypotheses. It is the part of scientific rigor to recognize hypothesis as hypothesis and then to make the most of it. Having accepted the fact that our observations and our self-evident truths do not together suffice to predict the future, we frame hypotheses to make up the shortage.

Calling a belief a hypothesis says nothing as to what the belief is about, how firmly it is held, or how well founded it is. Calling it a hypothesis suggests rather what sort of reason we have for adopting or entertaining it. A man adopts or entertains a hypothesis because it would explain, if it were true, some things that he already believes. Its evidence is seen in its consequences. For example, consider again the detective thriller in Chapter I. We were concerned in those pages with change of belief on the strength of new evidence. But how would we have reached, in the first place, the belief which the new evidence led us to abandon? It was a hypothesis. It was the belief that Cabot committed the murder, and it was, for a while, the best hypothesis we could devise to explain such circumstances as the killing, the undisturbed state of the victim's effects, the record of Abbott in the hotel register, and the testimony of Babbitt's brother-in-law. And then, when Cabot was discovered on television, what we did was to try to devise a plausible new hypothesis that would explain the enlarged array of circumstances.

Hypothesis, where successful, is a two-way street, extending back to explain the past and forward to predict the future. What we try to do in framing hypotheses is to explain some otherwise unexplained happenings by inventing a plausible story, a plausible description or history of relevant portions of the world. What to count as plausible here is a question not to be lightly answered —least of all in a book about belief and evidence. For the time being we may note five virtues which count toward plausibility, and which a hypothesis may enjoy in varying degrees.

Virtue I is *conservatism*. In order to explain the happenings that we are inventing it to explain, the hypothesis may have to conflict with some of our previous beliefs; but the fewer the better. Acceptance of a hypothesis is of course like acceptance of any belief in that it demands rejection of whatever conflicts with it. The less rejection of prior beliefs required, the more plausible the hypothesis—other things being equal. The plausibility of a hypothesis varies inversely with the plausibility of the prior beliefs that it disallows.

Virtue II is *generality*. The most celebrated triumph on this score was Newton's, when he showed how the elliptical paths of heavenly bodies and the parabolic paths of earthly projectiles could be accounted for by identical, general laws of motion. In order to achieve this generality he had to add a hypothesis of gravitation; and the generality gained justified adding it. Another famous triumph of this kind was achieved by Count Rumford and later physicists when they showed how the relation of gas pressure to temperature could be accounted for by the impact of oscillating particles, for in this way they reduced the theory of gases to the general laws of motion. In order to achieve this generality they had to add the hypothesis that gas consists of oscillating particles, or molecules; again, the generality gained justified adding it. Ordinarily no such staggering generality can be hoped for, but we do what we can. When we find electricity conducted by a piece of copper wire, we leap to the hypothesis that all copper, not just long thin copper, conducts electricity. Generality is a matter of degree.

The plausibility of a hypothesis depends largely on how compatible the hypothesis is with our being observers placed at random in the world. Funny coincidences often occur, but they are not the stuff that plausible hypotheses are made of. The more general the hypothesis is by which we account for our present observation, the less of a coincidence it is that our present observation should fall under it. Hence, in part, the power of Virtue II to confer plausibility.

The possibility of testing a hypothesis by repeatable experiment presupposes that the hypothesis has at least some share of Virtue II. For in a repetition of an experiment the test situation can never be exactly what it was for the earlier run of the experiment; and so, if both runs are to be relevant to the hypothesis, the hypothesis must be at least general enough to apply to both test situations.[1] One would of course like to have it much more general still.

[1] We are indebted to Nell E. Scroggins for suggesting this point.

A third virtue, without which Virtue II comes to little, is *simplicity*, Virtue III. When there are hypotheses to choose between, and their claims are equal except in respect of simplicity, we choose the one that looks simpler. Generality without simplicity is cold comfort. Thus, take celestial mechanics with its elliptical orbits, and take also terrestrial mechanics with its parabolic trajectories, just take them in tandem as a bipartite theory of motion. If the two together cover everything covered by Newton's unified laws of motion, then generality is no ground for preferring Newton's theory to the two taken together. But Virtue III, simplicity, is.

Where simplicity considerations become especially vivid is in drawing curves through plotted points on a graph. Consider the familiar practice of plotting measurements. Distance up the page represents altitude about sea level, for instance, and distance across represents the temperature of boiling water. We plot our measurements on the graph, one dot for each pair. However many points we plot, there remain infinitely many curves that may be drawn through them. Whatever curve we draw represents our generalization from the data, our prediction of what boiling temperatures would be found at altitudes as yet untested. And the curve we will choose to draw is the simplest curve that passes through, or reasonably close to, all the plotted points.

Science as a whole is a system of hypotheses that accommodates all observations to date, minus such ones as scientists have found it in their conscience to pass over (see Chapter II). There is a premium on simplicity in the hypotheses, but the highest premium is on simplicity in the giant joint hypothesis that is science, or the particular science, as a whole. We cheerfully sacrifice simplicity of a part for greater simplicity of the whole when we see a way of doing so.

What is simplicity? For curves we can make good sense of it in geometrical terms. A simple curve is continuous, and among continuous curves the simplest are perhaps those whose curvature changes most gradually from point to point. In most hypotheses, however, unlike those expressed by curves, the quality of simplicity seems disconcertingly subjective and psychological. One hypothesis will count as simpler than another if its grammatical structure is the same but its terms are more familiar; here the test of simplicity is a subjective one of familiarity. Or again perhaps one hypothesis counts as simpler than another if its grammatical structure is simpler; and even here the test is in a way subjective, since grammatical structure is only an accident of one or another language and not a direct reflection of nature. This subjectivity of simplicity is puzzling, if simplicity in hypotheses is to make for plausibility. Why should the subjectively simpler of two hypotheses stand a better chance of predicting objective events?

The policy of favoring simplicity does seem to work out well on the whole, and it is a policy that we have been following for a long time. Even primitive man doubtless tends to favor the simpler generalization in his expectations, if only because it is the one most likely to occur to him. We are not going to advise abandoning the policy now. But at the same time an essay on belief and evidence would be remiss in not speculating on the puzzle. How can subjective simplicity be relevant to prediction?

One suggestion is that the simpler a hypothesis is, the fewer ways there are for it to go wrong. This is unconvincing because of the vagueness of "ways." Our judgment that one hypothesis can go wrong in more ways than another depends on what we count as one way and what we count as two; and this matter is apt to be as subjective as our judgment that the one is less simple than the other. These could be just two ways of expressing the same feeling.

A more promising but more cynical suggestion is that when we keep score on the predictions based on our hypotheses, we score the simpler hypotheses more leniently. Again consider curves, where simplicity comparisons are so clear. If a curve is kinky and complex, and if some measurement predicted from the curve turns out to miss the mark by a distance as sizable as some of the kinks of the curve itself, we will count the prediction a failure. We will feel that so kinky a curve, if correct, would have had a kink to catch this wayward point. On the other hand, a miss of the same magnitude might be excused if the curve were smooth and simple. It might be excused as due to inaccuracy of measurement or to some unexplained local interference. This cynical doctrine of selective leniency is very plausible in the case of the curves. And we may reasonably expect a somewhat similar but less easily pictured selectivity to be at work in the interest of the simple hypotheses where curves are not concerned. Surely, however, this is not the whole story. The heightened plausibility of simple hypotheses is not wholly due to a juggling of the accounts.

Hypothesis

Casting about for a supplementary explanation of a less cynical kind, we find a hopeful suggestion in Darwin's theory of
natural selection. It offers a causal connection between subjective simplicity and objective truth in the following way. Innate
subjective standards of simplicity that make people prefer some
hypotheses to others will have survival value insofar as they
favor successful prediction. Those who predict best are likeliest
to survive and reproduce their kind, in a state of nature anyway,
and so their innate standards of simplicity are handed down.
Such standards will also change in the light of experience, be-
coming still better adapted to the growing body of science in the
course of the individual's lifetime. (But these improvements do
not get handed down genetically.)

On a problem of this depth and magnitude, perhaps the most
we can hope to accomplish in our speculations is to manifest a
respect for the problem. Supposing this accomplished by the
above speculation, let us return to another matter: the relations
between simplicity, or Virtue III, and other virtues. We saw that
Virtue II, generality, comes to little except in company with III.
Generality with simplicity is what we want. Between Virtue I,
conservatism, and the more radical pair, II and III, a certain
tension persists, as between the Right and the Left. When a way
is seen of gaining great generality with little loss of simplicity,
or great simplicity with no loss of generality, conservatism can
give way to scientific revolution.

The aftermath of the famous Michelson-Morley experiment of
1887 is a case in point. The purpose of this delicate and ingenious
experiment was to measure the speed with which the earth
travels through the ether. For two centuries, from Newton on-
ward, it had been a well entrenched tenet that something called
the ether pervaded all of what we think of as empty space. The
great physicist Lorentz (1853–1928) had hypothesized that the
ether itself was stationary. What the experiment revealed was
that the method that was expected to enable measurement of
the earth's speed through the ether was totally inadequate to that
task. Supplementary hypotheses multiplied in an attempt to
explain the failure without seriously disrupting the accepted
physics. Lorentz, in an effort to save the hypothesis of stationary
ether, shifted to a new and more complicated set of formulas in
his mathematical physics. Einstein soon cut through all this,
propounding what is called the special theory of relativity.

This was a simplification of physical theory. Not that Einstein's theory is as simple as Newton's had been; but Newton's physics had been shown untenable by the Michelson-Morley experiment. The point is that Einstein's theory is simpler than Newton's as corrected and supplemented and complicated by Lorentz and others. It was a glorious case of gaining simplicity at the sacrifice of conservatism; for the time-honored ether went by the board, and far older and more fundamental tenets went by the board too. Drastic changes were made in our conception of the very structure of space and time.

Yet let the glory not blind us to Virtue I. When our estrangement from the past is excessive, the imagination boggles; genius is needed to devise the new theory, and high talent is needed to find one's way about in it. Even Einstein's revolution, moreover, had its conservative strain; Virtue I was not wholly sacrificed. The old physics of Newton's classical mechanics is, in a way, preserved after all. For the situations in which the old and the new theories would predict contrary observations are situations that we are not apt to encounter without sophisticated experiment—because of their dependence on exorbitant velocities or exorbitant distances. This is why classical mechanics held the field so long. Whenever, even having switched to Einstein's relativity theory, we dismiss those exorbitant velocities and distances for the purpose of some practical problem, promptly the discrepancy between Einstein's theory and Newton's becomes too small to matter. Looked at from this angle, Einstein's theory takes on the aspect not of a simplification but a generalization. We might say that the sphere of applicability of Newtonian mechanics in its original simplicity was shown, by the Michelson-Morley experiment and related results, to be less than universal; and then Einstein's theory comes as a generalization, presumed to hold universally. Within its newly limited sphere, Newtonian mechanics retains its old utility. What is more, the evidence of past centuries for Newtonian mechanics even carries over, within these limits, as evidence for Einstein's physics; for, as far as it goes, it fits both.

What is thus illustrated by Einstein's relativity is more modestly exemplified elsewhere, and generally aspired to: the retention, in some sense, of old theories in new ones. If the new theory can be so fashioned as to diverge from the old only in ways that are undetectable in most ordinary circumstances, then it inherits the evidence of the old theory rather than having to overcome it. Such is the force of conservatism even in the context of revolution.

Hypothesis

Virtues I through III may be further illustrated by considering Neptune. That Neptune is among the planets is readily checked by anyone with reference material; indeed it passes as common knowledge, and there is for most of us no need to check it. But only through extensive application of optics and geometry was it possible to determine, in the first instance, that the body we call Neptune exists, and that it revolves around the sun. This required not only much accumulated science and mathematics, but also powerful telescopes and cooperation among scientists. As discoveries in astronomy go, this was an easy one; but it could not have been made at all without the large body of science already built.

In fact it happens that Neptune's existence and planethood were strongly suspected even before that planet was observed. Physical theory made possible the calculation of what the orbit of the planet Uranus should be, but Uranus' path differed measurably from its calculated course. Now the theory on which the calculations were based was, like all theories, open to revision or refutation. But here conservatism operates: one is loath to revise extensively a well established set of beliefs, especially a set so deeply entrenched as a basic portion of physics. And one is even more loath to abandon as spurious immense numbers of observation reports made by serious scientists. Given that Uranus had been observed to be as much as two minutes of arc from its calculated position, what was sought was a discovery that would render this deviation explicable within the framework of accepted theory. Then the theory and its generality would be unimpaired, and the new complexity would be minimal.

It would have been possible in principle to speculate that some special characteristic of Uranus exempted that planet from the physical laws that are followed by other planets. If such a hypothesis had been resorted to, Neptune would not have been discovered; not then, at any rate. There was a reason, however, for not resorting to such a hypothesis. It would have been what is called an *ad hoc* hypothesis, and ad hoc hypotheses are bad air; for they are wanting in Virtues II and III. Ad hoc hypotheses are hypotheses that purport to account for some particular observations by supposing some very special forces to be at work in the particular cases at hand, and not generalizing sufficiently beyond those cases. The vice of an ad hoc hypothesis admits of degrees. The extreme case is where the hypothesis covers only the observations it was invented to account for, so that it is totally useless in prediction. Then also it is insusceptible of confirmation, which would come of our verifying its predictions.

Another example that has something of the implausibility of an ad hoc hypothesis is the water-diviner's belief that a willow wand held above the ground can be attracted by underground water. The force alleged is too special. One feels, most decidedly, the lack of an intelligible mechanism to explain the attraction. And what counts as intelligible mechanism? A hypothesis strikes us as giving an intelligible mechanism when the hypothesis rates very well in Virtues I, II, and III: familiarity, generality, simplicity. We attain the ultimate in intelligibility of mechanism, no doubt, when we see how to explain something in terms of physical impact, or the familiar and general laws of motion.

There is an especially notorious sort of hypothesis which, whether or not properly classified also as ad hoc, shares the traits of insusceptibility of confirmation and uselessness in prediction. This is the sort of hypothesis that seeks to save some other hypothesis from refutation by systematically excusing the failures of its predictions. When the Voice from Beyond is silent despite the incantations of the medium, we may be urged to suppose that "someone in the room is interfering with the communication." In an effort to save the prior hypothesis that certain incantations will summon forth the Voice, the auxiliary hypothesis that untoward thoughts can thwart audible signals is advanced. This auxiliary hypothesis is no wilder than the hypothesis that it was invoked to save, and thus an uncritical person may find the newly wrinkled theory no harder to accept than its predecessor had been. On the other hand the critical observer sees that evidence has ceased altogether to figure. Experimental failure is being milked to fatten up theory.

These reflections bring a fourth virtue to the fore: *refutability*, Virtue IV. It seems faint praise of a hypothesis to call it refutable. But the point, we have now seen, is approximately this: some imaginable event, recognizable if it occurs, must suffice to refute the hypothesis. Otherwise the hypothesis predicts nothing, is confirmed by nothing, and confers upon us no earthly good beyond perhaps a mistaken peace of mind.

This is too simple a statement of the matter. Just about any hypothesis, after all, can be held unrefuted no matter what, by making enough adjustments in other beliefs—though sometimes doing so requires madness. We think loosely of a hypothesis as implying predictions when, strictly speaking, the implying is done by the hypothesis together with a supporting chorus of ill-distinguished background beliefs. It is done by the whole relevant theory taken together.

Properly viewed, therefore, Virtue IV is a matter of degree, as are its three predecessors. The degree to which a hypothesis partakes of Virtue IV is measured by the cost of retaining the hypothesis in the face of imaginable events. The degree is measured by how dearly we cherish the previous beliefs that would have to be sacrificed to save the hypothesis. The greater the sacrifice, the more refutable the hypothesis. A prime example of deficiency in respect of Virtue IV is astrology. The key here is that no amount of failure of prediction is allowed to count against the theory that the stars rule our destinies. If nothing else is available there is always some item of information, perhaps in the form of a planet's location at a long gone time, that may be alleged to have been overlooked.

A fifth virtue is perhaps worth noting still: Virtue V, *modesty*. The point here is that, other things being equal, the less story the better. Modesty falls indeed under conservatism, commonly so called. But by Virtue I we meant conservatism only in a literal sense—conservation of past beliefs. Thus there remain grades of modesty still to choose among even when Virture I—compatibility with previous beliefs—is achieved to perfection; for both a slight hypothesis and an extravagant one might be compatible with all previous beliefs. If someone rings our telephone, asks for an unknown party, and ends by apologizing for calling the wrong number, we will guess that he slipped in dialing; we will not likely embrace the more elaborate speculation that he was a burglar checking to see if anyone was home. Modesty enhances plausibility for the same reason, perhaps, that we grudgingly noted when discussing simplicity; namely, the more there is to a story, the more ways there are for it to be wrong.

Note however that modesty can also stand in a certain tension with simplicity. For, as in Einstein's case, the simplest of several alternatives may be the boldest. Modesty is in tension also, surely, with generality. But the point of Virtue V is just that our hypothesis should not be more elaborate than called for by the other virtues.

All our contemplating of special virtues of hypotheses will not, we trust, becloud the fact that the heart of the matter is observation. Virtues I through V are guides to the framing of hypotheses that, besides conforming to past observations, may plausibly be expected to conform to future ones. When they fail on the latter score, questions are reopened. Thus it was that the Michelson-Morley experiment led to modifications, however inelegant, of Newton's physics at the hands of Lorentz. When Einstein came out with a simpler way of accommodating past observations, moreover, his theory was no mere reformulation of the Newton-Lorentz system; it was yet a third theory, different in some of its predicted observations and answerable to them. Its superior simplicity brought plausibility to its distinctive consequences, as is the way of Virtue III and the other virtues.

Hypotheses were to serve two purposes: to explain the past and predict the future. Roughly and elliptically speaking, the hypothesis serves these purposes by implying the past events that it was supposed to explain, and by implying future ones. More accurately speaking, as we saw, what does the implying is the whole relevant theory taken together, as newly revised by adoption of the hypothesis in question. Moreover, the predictions that are implied are mostly not just simple predictions of future observations or other events; more often they are conditional predictions. The hypothesis will imply that we will make these further observations if we look in such and such a place, or take other feasible steps. If the predictions come out right, we can win bets or gain other practical advantages. Also, when they come out right, we gain confirmatory evidence for our hypotheses. When they come out wrong, we go back and tinker with our hypotheses and try to make them better.

What we called limiting principles in Chapter III are, when intelligible, best seen as hypotheses—some good, some bad. Similarly, of course, for scientific laws generally. And similarly for laws of geometry, set theory, and other parts of mathematics. All these laws—those of physics and those of mathematics equally—are among the component hypotheses that fit together to constitute our inclusive scientific theory of the world. The most general hypotheses tend to be the least answerable to any particular observation, since subsidiary hypotheses can commonly be juggled and adjusted to accommodate conflicts; and on this score of aloofness there is no clear boundary between theoretical physics and mathematics. Of course hypotheses in various fields of inquiry may tend to receive their confirmation from different kinds of investigation, but this should in no way conflict with our seeing them all as hypotheses.

We talk of framing hypotheses. Actually we inherit the main

ones, growing up as we do in a going culture. The continuity of belief is due to the retention, at each particular time, of most beliefs. In this retentiveness science even at its most progressive is notably conservative. Virtue I looms large. A reasonable man will look upon some of his retained beliefs as self-evident, on others as common knowledge though not self-evident, on others as vouched for by authority in varying degree, and on others as hypotheses that have worked all right so far.

But the going culture goes on, and each of us participates in adding and dropping hypotheses. Continuity makes the changes manageable. Disruptions that are at all sizable are the work of scientists, but we all modify the fabric in our small way, as when we conclude on indirect evidence that the schools will be closed and the planes grounded or that an umbrella thought to have been forgotten by one man was really forgotten by another.

EXERCISES

1. Cite some hypotheses that have been advanced both in and out of science and show how they fare with respect to this Chapter's five Virtues. Notice that Virtue I in particular depends on the stock of prior beliefs that is presupposed, and that all five, to one extent or another, are well thought of as attaching to a hypothesis in comparison with its thinkable alternatives rather than absolutely.

2. First think of a case that invites the framing of a hypothesis. Then frame for that case, for each of the five Virtues in turn, a hypothesis deficient in that one Virtue though adequate in the others. Finally, for the same case, find a hypothesis that has a goodly share of all five Virtues.

Chapter VI

Induction, Analogy, and Intuition

Why do we expect toothpaste to exude when we squeeze the tube? We could cite general principles about what happens to liquids or soft solids under pressure, but we are more likely to support our expectation in terms of our past experience with tubes and their squeezings. What happens in such simple activities is related to general principles only in ways which, for most of us, remain far in the background. Very far; for were toothpaste to fail to spurt forth on a given squeezing we would surely not want to rewrite our physics. We would consider such hypotheses as that the toothpaste in the tube had been used up, that it was blocked in its passage by some foreign object, or that it had hardened. We would explain a failure of our expectation in the least sweeping terms available, making the revision in our belief body as small as possible. We would maximize Virtues I and V of Chapter V: conservatism and modesty.

We expect the toothpaste mainly because prior squeezings have produced toothpaste. Such is very commonly the way of our expectations. We support our expectations—our beliefs about the future—by appeal to what is past. If Western sagas have always been seen to resolve their seemingly insuperable problems just moments before the end of scheduled air time, we expect the next Western saga we view to do so. If Bullwhip Fudgies have again and again, without fail, inserted their advertisement in the middle of the weekly Lionel Flemm Hour, we expect them to do so when next we tune in that program. Such expectation could indeed be forestalled, as by a newspaper headline "Bullwhip Unloads Flemm." Or we might simply be disappointed in our expectation on some occasion. Normally we are less than certain how things will go in the future, no matter how extensive our backlog of experience. Among the expectations that have their share of support are those that bid us brace for surprises.

More may contribute to our expectations than mere counting of cases. We perhaps come to see the rationale of the program's achieving resolution while air time, but not too much of it, lasts. Given what we suppose to be the purpose of its producers, what we have observed falls into a scheme of things. So it is with our beliefs pretty generally: they partially support one another by partially explaining one another. But, even so, what we come to believe derives much of its support from the sheer bulk of past cases. This simple and unimaginative source of belief is a factor that is central to the process of learning from experience and it needs to be isolated for consideration.

This central factor is the expectation that future cases will work out like past ones. It is the attribution of similar behavior to similar things. This familiar method of framing a general hypothesis, by generalizing from observed cases to all cases of the kind, is called *induction*.

When we try to be a bit more explicit and precise about induction's guiding principle—that future cases will be like past ones—we are suddenly lost in perplexity. The problem has been put in most striking form by the contemporary philosopher Nelson Goodman. Suppose that many emeralds have been examined for color and all have been found green. You may wonder how, failing greenness, we would know that they were emeralds in the first place; but this is not the point of the example. Imagine, so as to get on with Goodman's point, that emeralds have been identified in the dark by a chemical test, and that we are checking on color afterward. Very well, then; since all up to now have proved green, we expect the next emerald examined to be green. However, consider whether the following is a reason to the contrary, and, if not, why not. We adopt a new adjective, "grue," explained as follows: anything is grue if it is examined before midnight tonight, and is green, or else is not examined by then, and is blue. Thus the grue emeralds comprise all those green ones that will have been examined by midnight tonight together with all blue ones, if any, not examined by then. Now since all emeralds so far examined have been examined before midnight tonight, and have been green, it is also true that they have all been grue. We took their greenness to license our expectation that the next to be examined would be green; so then, symmetrically, their grueness should plump for the next one's grueness. Suppose that the next emerald to be examined will not be examined before midnight tonight. It, then, will have to be blue if it is to be grue. Thus we have a paradox: the next emerald is expected to be green since all emeralds examined have been green, but it is also expected to be grue, and therefore blue, since all emeralds examined have been grue.

There is no temptation to expect the next emerald to be blue. It is alarmingly difficult, however, to say why that inference is not legitimate while the inference to greenness is. What more clearly emerges is that to say that we expect future cases to be like past ones is, on its face, to say nothing.

This point is further borne out by a second paradox of induction. If we could fairly infer by induction that future cases will share each trait shared by all past ones, then there would be, for each of us, overwhelming inductive evidence for the solemn proposition that he is living his last moment. For, consider any specific moment. Say, for instance, that 1970 is about to begin. Every moment of one's life thus far has had the trait of being prior to 1970. By induction, then, may one conclude that all moments of one's life will share that trait? This conclusion, if correct, would be one's last.

And yet, if some illogician were to make a habit of these lugubrious inductions, he would find each time that the induction failed; he has always survived. A second-level induction, an induction about such inductions, tells him that such inductions are always wrong. Should he sigh with relief and conclude that he is immortal? He might even have reached this cheerful conclusion more directly, if he had begun in a sanguine frame of mind. For he could simply have observed that every past moment of his life had been followed by further living. By induction he might then have concluded that every moment of his life would be followed by further living, and hence that he would live forever.

The sober fact is that we cannot expect every trait shared by past cases to carry forward to future cases. Some traits command confident expectation of continuance and some do not. We expect greenness to carry forward to further emeralds; grueness not. We do not expect the trait of being prior to 1970 to carry forward to future moments without end, and neither do we expect the trait of being followed by further living to carry forward without end. Green is *projectible*, as Goodman says, while grue and these other traits are not. Induction projects the projectible traits into the future, and not the others.

To call a trait projectible is only to say that it is suited to induction, and not to say why. We may still ask why some traits should be thus suited, and how to spot them. We do have a natural knack for spotting such traits, with better than random success; they are the traits we notice. Green is a trait that we naturally and unhesitatingly project from past observation to future expectation; on the other hand the trait of being prior to 1970 is not such a one, and neither is the trait of being followed by further living, and neither is grue. It is significant that we did not have a word for grue; it is not a trait we notice.

Induction is the expectation that similar things will behave similarly; better, that things already seen to be appreciably similar will prove similar in further ways. The question what traits are projectible, then, can as well be put simply thus: What counts as similarity? Everything is similar to everything in some respect. Any two things share as many traits as any other two, if we are undiscriminating about what to call a trait; any two things are joint members of as many sets, at any rate, as any other two. When we call something more similar to one thing than to another, we are not counting shared traits indiscriminately; we are counting projectible traits. Sharing greenness counts for similarity; sharing grueness does not. Our eye for projectibility is our eye for similarity. These are two names for the same problem. In fact, similarity, projectibility, and simplicity are all of a piece. Projectible traits count as simpler than others, and the sharing of projectible traits counts as similarity.

Induction is not peculiarly intellectual. Essentially it is just a matter of learning from experience what to expect; and everyone is at it continually. Other animals are at it too, in learning what to avoid and where to go for food and water. All such learning proceeds by similarity, or projection of traits. All of it depends on a prior tendency to notice certain traits and so to single them out for projection rather than others. Our eye for similarity or projectibility is, at its crudest, part of our animal heritage. And why should it be so successful? Why should traits like green, which we have an innate tendency to notice and so to project, tend also to be the right ones—the ones that succeed in prediction? To this question, just as to the question of simplicity in Chapter V, the answer is surely natural selection. An innate sensitivity to certain traits, and insensitivity to others, has survival value insofar as the traits that are favored are favorable to prediction.

Our native flair for projectible traits does not remain as evolution left it. It develops further in the light of our experience. We can make inductive generalizations concerning the successes and failures of our past inductions, and so decide in effect that certain traits were not so projectible as we had thought. We revise some of our groupings. We read whales out of the tribe of fishes. We fix upon new traits in the light of a developing scientific theory, and find that inductions based on these traits are more successful. Science advances induction as induction advances science.

Induction is not a procedure alternative to hypothesis; it is a case of hypothesis. Induction is the natural avenue to Virtue II, generality. Virtue III, simplicity, is also always present where induction takes place, since projectible traits are felt as simpler than others. Induction is the way not to helter-skelter generality, or Virtue II alone, but to Virtues II and III combined.

According to traditional accounts, inference has two main species: deductive and inductive. Deductive is said to proceed from the more to the less general, inductive from the less to the more; so induction gives you more than you began with, deduction less. These were looked upon as complementary and symmetrical ways of justifying knowledge. To pair them thus and picture them as symmetrical, however, is to lose sight of serious differences. In Chapter III we reflected briefly on deductive inference as inference that can be carried out by a series of self-evident steps. Its central techniques are studied in logic and are well understood. Methods of inductive inference, on the other hand, are not sharply separable from strategies for framing hypotheses generally; and of such strategies no sharp and satisfactory theory is to be found, comparable to what logic provides for deduction. What little we shall have to say regarding the evaluation of inductive inference will appear in the next chapter, where we consider the confirmation and refutation of hypotheses.

Induction, we said, produces a hypothesis by generalization. This description supposes that the inductive conclusion is stated or thought as an explicit general law. Induction, we also said, is essentially just a matter of learning what to expect. But this description applies equally when a prediction or expectation is reached from past observations directly in a single leap, uninterrupted by an intervening general statement. Past experience in boiling lobsters leads us directly to expect the next one to turn red. Past experience with the dinner bell leads the dog directly to salivate at the sound of the gong, uninterrupted by an intervening general statement. We might reserve the term "induction" for inferences where the conclusion is general and explicit, since we have other terms for the leap from cases to cases. We have the term *analogy* and even *conditioned reflex*.

Thus the direct relation between our observation of the redness of past boiled lobsters and our expectation of redness of the next victim is a relation of analogy. The name of induction can be reserved for our generalization that *all* boiled lobsters are red. Again our individual expectations on television, and of the emergence of toothpaste from the squeezed tube, are got by analogy. The corresponding inductions, or general hypotheses, would in ordinary circumstances never be framed at all.

One who derives a belief by analogy need not be prepared to offer any inductive support for it nor even notice that his belief rests on an analogy. It is the way of each of us most of the time to forge new beliefs from old ones without reflecting at all on the arguments that might be summoned in their behalf. Such beliefs may still be eminently reasonable. We form habits of building beliefs much as we form our other habits; only in habits of building beliefs there is less room for idiosyncrasy.

Some analogies that we use are notoriously weak. Perhaps a person hears a new voice and, noticing that the voice resembles that of an old friend, speculates that the voice's owner will be like the old friend in other significant ways. Such an analogy is shadowy, but we all tend at times to build on analogies that are no better. When a feature of a newly encountered person or object strikes a familiar chord it is often fairly instinctive to project to the new person or object what experience has associated with that feature. As a person gains in experience he learns, or should learn, to temper such expectations. He learns to discriminate between associations that are worth building new beliefs on and those that are not. The more people he meets the better he is able to judge what expectations he can base on a person's voice. His native flair for projectibility is developing in the light of experience and even so he may remain quite unable to articulate any principles for his acquired discrimination. It is much easier to build beliefs and hypotheses than to describe the rationale behind their construction. This is true even where the hypotheses belong to science.

Sometimes, though we are quite convinced that a belief is right, we can think of no reasons at all for holding it. It is in such cases that we are apt to give credit to *intuition*. Some people think of intuition as a mystical source of knowledge—a source disconnected from other ways of reaching conclusions. Happily it need not be so regarded. Consider a situation in which we sense that a person is insincere. There may be no known evidence for the belief, but that need not mean that no relevant observations have been made. Perhaps the person hesitated just a fraction of a second before answering some question, or perhaps he momentarily exhibited a certain facial expression. Such things might well have been what led to our suspicion about him, even though they may never have registered as data. This would be unconscious analogy at work. Our sensing insincerity could rest on our picking up a sensory clue like one once linked with someone believed to be insincere. Not only might we not have noticed the clue; we may even have forgotten the former attribution of insincerity.

Some beliefs that might be credited to intuition by one person would be otherwise credited by another. If the businessman's wife distrusts her husband's prospective client, it is intuition; if her husband distrusts him, it is experience.

Where an intuition has anything at all to be said for it, it has something making no mention of intuition to be said for it: sensory clues that may not have registered as such, long forgotten beliefs, analogies more or less vague. Uncovering the basis of such a belief helps us to appraise the belief; yet to demand that the basis of every reasonable belief be thus uncovered would be to demand the impossible. Think of our everyday ability to recognize people we know on sight. We may be totally incapable of giving enough description of a person we know well to enable anyone else to recognize him. We just have this uncanny knack. Still no one is inclined to say that we recognize our friends through intuition; it is vaguely set down to experience. We respond to visual clues, organize them in a twinkling, and compare the result with what is stored in memory.

That last phrase is one that is common in talk of computers.

And indeed, machines are able to perform certain tasks of recognition. For example, machines can be programmed to discriminate handwritten letters of the alphabet, so that they can read script as well as printing. We know how they do it; they compare what is fed into them with what has been internalized in them through programming. The study of such devices belongs to the field called artificial intelligence, which studies how tasks that would normally be thought to require intelligent behavior might be carried out by machines. It seems likely that development of this field will lead to significant gains in psychology. In particular, it should bring heightened understanding of how humans recognize complex objects.

Analogy can lead not only from particular experiences to particular expectations, but also from general hypotheses to general hypotheses. Say we have evidence that a serum prepared from a certain bacterial culture immunizes against the disease caused by those bacteria. If there is a closely related disease caused by bacteria that we regard as very much like those causing the first disease, then we may find it plausible that a correspondingly prepared serum will immunize against the second disease. Our belief about the first serum has its claim to Virtue II, generality, enhanced if it is extensible to a similar belief about a similar serum. So even in advance of any testing we have reason to look favorably upon the hypothesis about the second serum. What is at work here is still analogy, but it is analogy now between two parallel laws rather than between particulars.

We pictured analogy as by-passing inductive generalizations; as moving directly from similars to similars. Now when the analogy is between general laws there is still the by-passed inductive generalization, which one might afterward try to capture. In the above example, the generalization would be a comprehensive law to the effect that immunity against each disease of a certain described class is conferred by a serum prepared from the corresponding bacteria. The class would be described by making explicit the similarities that related the two diseases in the original analogy; the class would include all diseases thus related.

Analogy as thus far pictured is an inferential leap, whereof the top of the trajectory is a slurred-over induction. The intervening generalization is slurred over because interest happens to be centered rather upon some particular instance that is to be inferred. Another effect of this allocation of interest is that we are likely to attend to more varied features of the instance that is to be inferred than we would if generality were our objective. Hence the previous instances or premises, from which we are making the analogical inference, are apt to have been so chosen as to share a variety of features with the case to be inferred. On this account we commonly have to make do with just one previous instance, as in the serum example, unlike the style of proper induction; and the single instance is apt moreover to carry sufficient conviction, thanks to the multiple resemblances. Thus it is that an analogy often looks very unlike a slurred-over induction, and the missing generalization is not always easy to supply.

The word "analogy" is of course often correctly applied to matters other than inference. It is applied to a common way of learning new terms. The concept of a class or set, for instance, is grasped by partial analogy to a heap, and the concept of an atom or electron is grasped by partial analogy to a visible speck. These other uses of the word "analogy" need not concern us. The common core of all the uses is fairly well covered by "similarity" or "parallelism."

EXERCISES

1. Think of some varied cases in which you have arrived at reasonable beliefs mainly through induction. Think of some contrasting examples in which straightforward inductions would have led to untoward hypotheses.

2. Think of some varied cases in which you have arrived at reasonable beliefs mainly through analogy. In each case try to articulate a plausible induction that might have served as "top of the trajectory." Contrive to include among your examples some for which such articulation is easy and some for which it is very difficult.

3. Examine some cases in which either you or others have looked upon some realization or suspicion as due to intuition. Construct plausible hypotheses about what might have grounded such realizations or suspicions.

4. To appreciate better the point about our uncanny knack, try to write a description of some person you know that would enable someone who does not know that person to recognize him or her. Play fair by choosing a person who exhibits no truly extraordinary visible features and by writing your description without peeking at either the person or a picture of the person.

Chapter VII

Confirmation
and Refutation

An author of this book experienced headaches accompanied by blurred vision. The first step in trying to find a way of preventing them was to find some explanation. Through a combination of recollection and watchfulness he came to suspect that the headaches were associated with eating sweet pickles, so he framed the hypothesis that the sweet pickles brought on the headaches. Once after thinking of this hypothesis he deliberately indulged himself in sweet pickles, and, to be sure, a headache followed. Abstention from such indulgence was found to coincide with absence of such headaches. He has accepted the hypothesis ever since, avoided sweet pickles, and had no such headaches.

The obvious way of testing a hypothesis is to test its consequences. One sees whether a headache follows the eating of sweet pickles, being prepared to discard, or at least modify, the hypothesis if none does. When a headache does follow, the hypothesis receives confirmation. But its truth is far from established thereby. It has merely withstood one challenge. We noted in Chapter V that many curves may be drawn through plotted points. This means that no matter how many data we have there will still be many mutually incompatible hypotheses each of which implies those data. What confirms one hypothesis will confirm many; the data are good for a whole sheaf of hypotheses and not just one. This is what makes it necessary for us to have criteria for hypotheses, such as the five Virtues of Chapter V, above and beyond the requirement that they should imply what we have observed. In terms of the Virtues a hypothesis may excel its rivals sufficiently to be regarded as definitely established.

Confirmation of the pickles hypothesis might have been pursued further. For one thing, the single experiment provided very limited confirmation for the hypothesis; further tests, in varied circumstances, might have been undertaken that would either have brought added confirmation or shown the hypothesis to be mistaken. For another thing, the hypothesis settled on might seem somewhat short on Virtue II, generality, since it gives no hint as to why one person should so react while other persons appear not to. Thus our sufferer might have sought a refinement of the hypothesis—a refinement that would account for his idiosyncrasy, perhaps by relating particular physiological traits to specific allergic reactions. In view of the sparseness of medical knowledge about such relationships, this would have been hard. Still, a certain plausibility can be claimed for the hypothesis on account of elementary background knowledge—the knowledge that what one eats often brings on unwelcome physical reactions. We build on what we know in order to learn more. Doing this maximizes the chance of finding a workable hypothesis that fits in with the rest of what we accept; thus it serves Virture I, conservatism. And since using what we already know may lighten the burden on the hypothesis sought and allow it to be a modest one, Virtue V may be served as well.

The pickles hypothesis was imprecise, as are many that suit our everyday purposes. It was imprecise in that it specified no required quantity of sweet pickles and no particular time interval between indulgence and reaction. And the terms in which it was cast were vague, since there can be doubt as to what is to count as a sweet pickle or as a headache of the appropriate kind.

Ordinarily, hypotheses used in science are more precise and less vague than those adopted in everyday affairs. There is for instance the scientific hypothesis or law about the boiling point of water, which says that water free of impurities boils at 100° C. if it is subject to a pressure of 760 millimeters. Measurement itself is of course never wholly precise; but what this hypothesis is meant to give us to expect is that you can bring the boiling point as near as you please to 100° C. by bringing the pressure closer and closer to 760 millimeters and also progressively purifying the water.

Precision might be listed as Virtue VI, supplementary to the five virtues in Chapter V. Like those virtues, precision conduces to the plausibility of a hypothesis. It does so in an indirect fashion. The more precise a hypothesis is, the more strongly it is confirmed by each successful prediction that it generates. This is because of the relative improbability of coincidences. If a prediction based on a hypothesis just happens to come out true for irrelevant reasons, that is a coincidence; and, the more precise a hypothesis, the less room there is for such a coincidence. If the hypothesis says precisely that the pickles will bring a headache in twelve to thirteen minutes, a confirmatory headache cannot be dismissed lightly as coincidence. If, on the other hand, the hypothesis just says vaguely that the pickles will bring a headache in the fullness of time, an eventual headache is as may be.

It might seem that precision opposes generality, but this is not so. Often when we widen a hypothesis we give up some precision, but this is only because we lack precise information over the wider domain, and not because such information is excluded in principle.

Precision comes mainly with the measuring of quantities, as the two foregoing examples illustrate. A notable boon of injecting quantity into hypotheses is *concomitant variation*, or *functional dependence*. Change the pressure from 760 millimeters to a lower or higher figure, and you change the boiling point of water from 100° C. to a correspondingly lower or higher figure. Once such a hypothesis is devised, describing the fluctuation of one quantity explicitly as some function of the fluctuation of another quantity, the confirmatory power of a few successful predictions is overwhelming.

Measure is not the sole source of precision. Another way of increasing precision is redefinition of terms. We take a term that is fuzzy and imprecise and try to sharpen its sense without impairing its usefulness. In so sharpening we may effect changes in the term's application; a new definition may let the term apply to some things that it did not formerly apply to, and it may keep the term from applying to some of the things to which it had applied. The idea is to have any changes come in harmless cases, so that precision is gained without loss. It is to be noted that hypotheses briefly expressible in everyday terms and purporting to have broad application rarely turn out to be unexceptionable. This is even to be expected, since everyday terms are mainly suited for everyday affairs, where lax talk is rife.

When philosophers give a precise sense to what was formerly a fuzzy term or concept it is called *explication* of that term or concept. Successful explications have been found for the concepts of deduction, probability, and computability, to name just three. It is no wonder that philosophers seek explications; for explications are steps toward clarity. But philosophers are not alone in this.

Biologists gained precision and something more when they gave the common term "fish" a sharp definition that banned whales; for the new distinction turned on biological characteristics that entered elsewhere into theory. Physicists made similar gains when they redefined such terms as "momentum" and "energy." Looking in another direction, we find judicial decisions contributing to the sharpening of legal concepts even without recourse to explicit definitions. Decisions regarding contracts, fraud, and conspiracy, for example, may give new guidelines for determining the range of those concepts. In English law the practice is to use old decisions as criteria as long as possible, and then, when old lines fail, to draw finer lines through fresh decisions.

Let us turn back now for a further look at confirmation. Virtues I through VI, though they give reasons to believe a hypothesis, are not called confirmation; this term is used more narrowly, for confirmation in subsequent experience. What confirms a hypothesis, insofar as it gets confirmed, is the verification of its predictions. When, more particularly, the hypothesis is a generalization arrived at by induction, those predictions are simply instances of the generalization. Thus what confirm an induction are its instances. Each green emerald confirms, in its small way, the induction that all emeralds are green.

But not every generalization is confirmed by its instances. This was the lesson of Goodman's contrived example of the grue emeralds. One or a thousand grue emeralds, inspected before the pivotal midnight, count none toward confirming the generalization that all emeralds are grue. Grue is not projectible. "All emeralds are grue," is not fair game for induction. In a word, "All emeralds are grue," is not *lawlike*. A lawlike general sentence is one whose instances count toward its confirmation; hence one couched in projectible predicates. Such sentences are called lawlike, rather than laws, in order not to demand that they be true.

At this point a technical refinement needs passing notice. Just as the instances of "All emeralds are green" are the green emeralds, so the instances of "All ungreen things are nonemeralds," are the ungreen nonemeralds—for instance, chickens. Now since chickens count none toward confirmation of the sentence "All emeralds are green," they must also count none toward confirmation of "All ungreen things are nonemeralds"; for these two sentences are logically equivalent (they logically imply each other). Therefore, the sentence "All ungreen things are nonemeralds" fails of lawlikeness, if lawlike sentences are defined simply as general sentences that are confirmed by their instances. Still this conclusion is intolerable, since the sentence is equivalent to the law "All emeralds are green." This quandary was propounded by the contemporary philosopher Carl G. Hempel. A way around it is to widen the definition of lawlikeness by saying that the lawlike sentences comprise not just the general sentences that are confirmed by their instances, but also all logical equivalents of such sentences.

In practice we seem to be able to recognize projectibility to our own satisfaction, and therewith lawlikeness, in most cases. Clear examples of lawlike sentences are "Whenever my toe hurts it rains," "All undergraduate courses have final examinations," "Every hydrogen molecule contains two atoms," and "Intensity of light varies inversely with the square of its source's distance." (Remember that a sentence need not be true to be lawlike.) A pair of sentences closer to borderline might be "All the coins in my pocket on Monday were dimes" and "Every coin I will receive in change next year will have been minted after 1929." The first of this pair appears to fall short of the line, since it is doubtful that verification of any one instance makes any other more likely; the second of the pair could pass as lawlike. Our readiness to draw the distinction in practice, in so many cases, is simply a manifestation of our flair for projectible traits; and we surmised in Chapter VI that this flair is in part an inherited result of evolution.

A lawlike generalization, then, is confirmed by each of its instances. An instance does not of course clinch the generalization, but each instance adds to the plausibility of it. A generalization with even a single false instance, on the other hand, is irremediably false. Any hypothesis, indeed any statement at all, that implies a falsehood is itself false. This asymmetry is pure logic: what implies a truth may be true or false, but what implies a falsehood is false.

It would appear to be easier, therefore, to refute a false hypothesis than to establish a true one. If a hypothesis implies observations at all, we may stand ready to drop the hypothesis as false as soon as an observation that it predicts fails to occur. In fact, however, the refutation of hypotheses is not that simple. We already know this from what was said in Chapter V regarding Virtue IV, refutability; there is the matter of the supporting chorus. It is not the contemplated hypothesis alone that does the implying, but rather that hypothesis and a supporting chorus of background beliefs. Nor is it usually a simple observation that is implied, but rather a conditional prediction that if a certain step is taken the observation will ensue. Discarding any particular hypothesis is just one of many ways of maintaining consistency in the face of a contrary observation; there are in principle many alternative ways of setting our beliefs in order.

Thus, consider again the hypothesis that pure water under 760 millimeters pressure boils at 100° C. Suppose that a quantity of what we take to be very pure water under a pressure of very nearly 760 is found to boil at 92° C. What conflict are not merely (a) the hypothesis and (b) the boiling at 92° C. Two further parties to the conflict immediately stand forth: the belief that (c) the water was pure and (d) the pressure was close enough to 760. Discarding the hypothesis is one way of maintaining consistency, but there are other ways. In the imagined case, of course, no scientist would reject the hypothesis, because it is such a highly accredited part of chemistry. Instead he would challenge (b), (c), or (d), each of which is open to question. In fact (b), (c), and (d) each rest in turn on some physics or chemistry, through the methods we use for determining what the temperature and pressure of a given liquid are, and when a liquid comes to a boil, and whether a liquid is pure water. So more than observation has entered into our acceptance of (b), (c), and (d). And even if we question no general beliefs underlying (b), (c), and (d), there could be some mistaken reading of dials and gauges. What has come to grief in our example is a whole family of beliefs. Sometimes when this happens it is relatively clear which members of the family are best rejected, and sometimes not—as witness the case of Abbott, Babbitt, and Cabot in Chapter I.

Confirmation and Refutation

We often speak of certain observations as consequences of a hypothesis. However, on more careful study we invariably find them to be consequences not of that hypothesis alone, but of the hypothesis together with other assumptions that we make. And the more precise the hypothesis the more likely this is; for the tighter its specifications are, the more techniques and previously accepted beliefs we need in order to see that the specifications are met. In the hypothesis just considered we needed techniques for determining, *inter alia*, that the water was pure and the pressure close enough to 760 millimeters. Our method for showing a hypothesis false turns out to be a method only for showing that something we have used is wrong—maybe the hypothesis under test and maybe some other belief.

Precise hypotheses, we see, are hard to isolate for testing. They tend to carry other beliefs with them. Imprecise ones, on the other hand, can be hard to test because of difficulty in determining exactly what they imply. The pickles hypothesis may be seen as an example of that. Again "Water boils at 100° C.," taken without its sharp conditions, must be seen as too incomplete for appraisal, if not just false outright.

Some philosophers of science have tried to apply numerical probabilities to hypotheses. This move is suggested by the reflection that confirmation is a matter of more and less. In games of chance, indeed, the probability of hypotheses makes good sense; in fact, this is where the calculus of probabilities began. There is a clear reason to assign a probability of 1 in not quite 505 to the hypothesis that your next poker hand will be a pat flush. It is clear what information to use in this computation; for we know what cards are in the deck and that you will receive five, while we do not know the order of the cards nor any other influences. This available information consequently reduces the question to a count of combinations. In the wider world, however, how could we begin to calculate the probability of a hypothesis—say of the hypothesis that the universe began with a bang, or that Babbitt was the murderer? There would be the problem of cataloguing all relevant information. Also there would be the far greater problem, which seems hopeless on the face of it, of compartmenting all alternative possibilities into what could be viewed as equal bits, preparatory to counting combinations. For the foreseeable future we can do no better on the whole, regarding the degree of confirmation of our hypotheses, than regard some as better confirmed than others and some as not comparable in those terms at all. This we must all see as the practical situation; and some philosophers see it also as the necessary situation in principle. C. S. Peirce, writing of induction, expressed the point thus:

> It may be conceived, and often is conceived, that induction lends a probability to its conclusion. Now that is not the way in which induction leads to the truth. It lends no definite probability to its conclusion. It is nonsense to talk of the probability of a law, as if we could pick universes out of a grab-bag and find in what proportion of them the law held good . . . What induction does (namely, to commence a proceeding which must in the long run approximate to the truth) . . . is infinitely more to the purpose.[1]

Cases do sometimes arise, even outside the gambling hells, where we can make reasonable sense of the probability of a hypothesis. Statistics up to now show, let us suppose, that inoculation against some particular disease has been effective in 93 percent of the cases in which it was used. This makes sense of assigning the probability of 93 percent to the hypothesis that Zee, recently inoculated and subsequently exposed, will escape the disease. It makes sense only relative, of course, to an agreed limitation of information; in this it is like the hypothesis of your getting a pat flush in your next hand. Customary terminology here is haphazard. The Zee example would be called a prediction, a probable prediction, because it is so specific and its probability is so high. The example of your next receiving a flush would not be called a prediction because, though it is equally specific, its probability is so low. It would just be called a slim chance. Anyway, both are hypotheses, and they are alike in their specificity and verifiability and unlike in their probability.

What is more worth noticing is that the hypotheses to which it makes clearest sense to assign probabilities seem to run thus to specificity. Furthermore there is always the need to decide what background information is to be taken into consideration. Different ways of setting this limitation can give different probabilities. Given that 60 percent of the registered voters in Wolf-whistle County are registered as Democrats, we might take it as 60 percent likely that Mr. Ledgington, known to be registered there, is a Democrat. Given instead that 80 percent of the membership of the National Tycoon Society is registered Republican, and that Ledgington is a member, we come out rather with a probability of 20 percent at best. Given the two data

[1] *Collected Papers*, vol. 2 (Cambridge, Mass.: Harvard, 1960), pp. 499–500.

together, and no others, we come out with neither figure; indeed, we are then hard put to it to estimate the probability.

The question—in the general case a forlorn one—of the probability of a hypothesis is not to be confused with the curious matter of a hypothesis of probability: a *statistical hypothesis*. An example of the latter would be the hypothesis that 51 percent of all children born are male, or that inoculations next year will prove 93 percent successful. These statistical hypotheses are of course just numerical hypotheses. Indeed, the second one is essentially just a prediction, which can be pretty well checked in a few years. Hypotheses of the same sort are commonly expressed more vaguely in ordinary language with help of such words as "usually," "many," and "most." But there are also hypotheses in modern physics that are statistical in a more stubborn and less trivial way. The behavior of elementary particles is in certain respects random in principle, according to quantum mechanics. But this is a realm of theory into which, despite its importance, we shall not presume to try to induct the reader.

EXERCISES

1. Tell about some case (like the headaches one) in which you successfully sought an explanation for purposes of prevention. If possible, take as your case one in which your first attempts at explanation proved unsuccessful. Explore the rationale by which you settled on the explanation finally adopted.

2. Take some everyday hypotheses that you accept and recast them as hypotheses that are very precise. Along with aiming at precision, your objective in recasting each hypothesis should be to keep its range of application as wide as possible while minimizing the likelihood of its meeting with counter-instances. (It is to be expected that there will have to be some narrowing of the range of application if the risk of counter-instance is to be kept from soaring.)

3. Think of some more generalizations that lie near the border-line between being lawlike and not. For each one tell on which side of the line you would incline toward placing it, and why.

4. Give some further illustrations of the role of the chorus of background beliefs in the testing of a hypothesis. Choose cases from both science and the workaday world.

Chapter VIII

Explanation

Seen from a certain angle, general hypotheses or laws are explanations. They explain the observations that they imply. This they do as far as they go, which is not generally as far as we could wish; for explanation, like peanuts, nourishes a desire for more of the same. We may respond to an explanatory law with a wish for a wider and deeper law to explain that law, and so on out.

Imagine a tribe, isolated enough to be unaffected by what we think of as the history of science, that migrates from an inland place to a seacoast. We may expect the tribesmen to become aware of the tides in short order, and if they are at all observant they will soon notice that the tides and the moon's position are related. In particular, they may find what is true of many coastal places to be true of theirs: that just after the moon is overhead the tide is high. This much is already a law, though by our standards a meagre one. It would be an easy law for them to come upon, given a little observation, and it could be expected to gain confirmation readily. We are assuming that the tribe has settled by a port whose establishment is small—which is to say a port where high tide comes while the moon is high.

Explanation

If some of our tribesmen are curious and observant they will improve their little law. They will correlate positions of the moon with low tides, and they will learn when to expect high tide while the moon is out of sight. They will notice that the high tide that comes moonlessly is a higher tide than the one with the moon overhead. In time they should recognize that the tides are maximized, both high and low, when the moon is new or full.

Even if they are too artless at first to formulate their discoveries, it should not take many months (or moons) for some of our tribesmen to learn to infer from the moon's position and phase a reasonable approximation of the water level. Then they can make predictions as of how high the water will be when next the moon is full and high. It may take longer for them to discover that there are deviations from their scheme—deviations that we trace to changes in the moon's distance and declination. Although rough, what they have may surely be seen as a law; and with it they have an explanation for the observed tides.

We may see their explanation as less than the best one that might be found, and not only because, at the outset anyway, it is founded on hypotheses that are inexact. For the explanation leaves unanswered the question *why* the moon relates to the tides as it does. (Neither does it make any mention of the relationship between the sun's position and the tides, but much of that is covered by attention to the moon's phases.) Now to ask why the moon and tides are related is to ask for a further explanation —an explanation of the law that the tribesmen have discovered. If there happens to be one among the tribesmen with the genius of a Newton, some version of the law of gravitation might be thought of. Such a law would then explain the lesser law, much as that one explained the observed tides. And it would also make for a deeper and more powerful explanation of the tides themselves. For, given enough data about the masses of the moon, sun, earth, and sea and their relative positions at given times, the tidal phenomena would be deducible. Actually there are problems involved in thus calculating tides; theoretically derived values can run afoul of the particular contours of ocean beds and beaches and even the flexibility of the earth. But if we can imagine there to have been a Newton among the tribesmen, we can also imagine there to have been capable geologists and oceanographers with whose help the needed extra factors can have been allowed for in calculation.

Even this degree of success need not be the last word as far as explanation is concerned. The tribesmen could, like physicists now, seek an even more powerful law or set of laws—say a unified field theory—under which the gravitation law might be subsumed in turn. In principle there is never a limit to what one can seek explanations for, since any explanation will itself contain lawlike sentences that might be subjects for further explanation. Of course, given our particular purposes, we may rest satisfied with some explanation as telling us all we want to know. But, as every parent can attest, the question "Why?" can still be asked no matter how much of a story has been told.

Explanation and prediction are roughly correlative. Since an explanation implies what it explains, it would have sufficed for prediction if it had been what we started with. Conversely, most knowledge that sanctions a prediction serves also as an explanation for what it predicts if what it predicts comes true.

The search for an explanation centers on the search for a credible hypothesis. We seek a hypothesis from which, perhaps with help from our other beliefs, what we want explained is deducible. The more plausible the hypothesis the more plausible the explanation. What will be acceptable as an explanation in a given case will depend on our interests and on how sophisticated we are about the subject at hand. We may be looking for our explanation in order to be able to control or prevent something, as with the headaches of Chapter VII; or our interest may lie in being able to predict certain events, as might have been the purpose of our tribesmen in trying to learn laws about the tides; or we may simply want to increase our understanding of something quite apart from any immediate practical concern.

Explanations, when we find them, can broaden our knowledge and so our capabilities. The law of gravitation was first heralded as explaining such things as planetary motions, the moon's effect on the tides, and the law of falling bodies. Later it turned out to have wider applications. It was a step toward a physical science which gave rise to rocket projection, to cite one offshoot. So a clearer picture of explanation can be expected to deepen our understanding of how our knowledge grows.

What kind of thing is subject to explanation? According to common talk it is frequently events and actions that receive explanations. Yet no explanation for an event can explain everything about that event, since of any event there is unlimitedly much that is true. What is really to be explained is not the event but rather something particular about it. This is usually blurred

in our ordinary talk, for this interesting reason: In saying what
it is that we want explained we do not merely designate some
event or action, we characterize it. If Caesar shouts "The die is
cast," an explanation might be requested either for his shouting
or for his claiming that the die was cast. The action or event in
question is one and the same, but the diverse characterizations
that mark the requests make them requests for explanations of
different things. So it cannot be simply the event or action for
which explanation is sought.

What recommends itself is a move reminiscent of one we
made back in Chapter I: we can think of our explanations as
explanations of sentences, or, more elaborately and accurately,
of the truth of those sentences. We may seek an explanation for
the truth of "He shouted" or for the truth of "He claimed that the
die was cast," for example. Once this is understood, however,
there is no need to harp on this way of construing explanations;
we may safely lapse into speaking more idiomatically, say of
explanations for his shouting and for his claiming what he did.

As a step toward explicating "explanation," we might say that
an explanation is a family of sentences that implies what we
want explained. Taking an explanation thus inclusively saves
mentioning the possible need for various of our other beliefs as
aids in deducing what we want; whatever such beliefs are needed
can simply be counted as part of the family. Thus, going back
to our seaside tribe, let us suppose that these people have become able to explain any observed tide by means of a family of
sentences consisting of (a) a formulation of their law relating
tides to lunar position and phase, and (b) data about lunar
position and phase at the time of the tide. (We imagine them to
have learned to infer what they need of (b) for cases where the
moon is below the horizon.) The law in (a) would be felt as the
essence of the explanation. In giving an explanation one often
omits mention of specific data and cites only what is thought to
be the relevant law or laws. That is reasonable enough if the data
are not themselves in doubt. If we are all aware that the moon
is on the horizon, then the mention of a law relating the tide to
this position of the moon will be enough, practically speaking, to
explain the tide. In giving explanations, as in offering arguments,
we normally render explicit only what we think may not be
known to those we are addressing. We leave the obvious unstated.
But an obvious premise, even if unstated, may still be part of
an argument; and so may an unstated belief constitute part of

an explanation. The question is what would have to be stated for the argument or explanation to be rendered in full. So it is quite in order to count the lunar data as part of the tribe's explanation.

Still, we cannot count just any family of sentences that implies what we want explained as an explanation of it. This would count every sentence as its own explanation, since, trivially, every sentence implies itself. We must demand rather that the explanation imply more; more must be deducible from it than just what was to be explained. We owe to a Molière comedy the classical violation of this tenet: asked why opium induces sleep, the doctor explains that it has a *virtus dormitiva*.

Of course this requirement of added scope on the part of explanations must not be met by the easy and evasive expedient of just annexing some arbitrary further truths to it. To plug this loophole we might stipulate that a family of sentences does not count as an explanation of a given sentence unless the deduction of that sentence requires use of every sentence in the family. Strictly, this plug is still inadequate because of possible trickery with compound sentences. However, we shall not pursue such technicalities here. Let us just leave our two antitriviality stipulations in this somewhat vague state: the explanation must imply more than what was to be explained, but each part of the explanation, short of the whole, must fall short of implying what was to be explained. Note incidentally that together the two stipulations prevent an explanation from containing the sentence explained.

Still, there are other ways in which our budding account of explanation may seem to be at odds with the common concept. One objection might be that our account fails to require that an explanation enhance understanding. It may seem, for example, that the general truth that anyone who drinks Dormiseltzer promptly falls asleep does not explain why a particular person who drank it fell asleep. "Why did I fall asleep when I drank my Dormiseltzer, Mommy?" "Because everyone who drinks it does." Admittedly, this answer may fail to enhance understanding; but it may fail only for special reasons. Certainly in the sweet pickles case the discovery that everyone who ate them suffered headaches would have been very much to the point. In the present example, dissatisfaction with the explanation may merely show that what was sought in the first place was an explanation of more than the one case of falling asleep. The request might be an idiomatic way of asking for an explanation of the very law that came as response: "Everyone who drinks it does." If so, no wonder the response seemed unsatisfactory.

Often the search for an explanation is the search for a cause. Thus, suppose that what is to be explained is that Bullwhip Fudgies went up two points on Monday. By the standard of explanation proposed above, it would count as an explanation to say that Tuesday's paper said so and that the financial page is generally accurate. Such an explanation would command little interest among students of the stock market, precisely because it shuns causes. The notion of cause, notwithstanding the philosophical attention it has had, leaves much clarity to be desired; but one clear point about it is that the cause is not later than the effect. A related point is that knowledge of the cause confers foreknowledge of the effect; and this, if the truth were known, is what gnaws at the heart of the student of the stock market.

If the question had been, not why Bullwhip went up, but how we knew, then our newspaper reference would have seemed a natural explanation. Our version of explanation does not adequately separate evidence from cause. Moreover, the state of the notion of cause being what it is, we do not see our way to repairing this fault satisfactorily.

A further problem arises in the case of statistical explanations. Say that Zee is exposed to a contagious disease but fails to contract it. Zee may wonder why. If he discovers that he was once inoculated against the disease, he may accept this as an explanation, provided that he also believes that a high percentage of those so inoculated are rendered immune to it. But that percentage need not be 100; that is, Zee might believe that some who are inoculated remain susceptible to the disease, but that he happens, luckily, not to be among them. In that case what was offered as an explanation fails to meet the requirement of implying what was to be explained. On this score our criterion for explanation proves relatively strict, demanding firmer grounds than we are sometimes willing to make do with. For this example we could, however, lean toward a fully lawlike explanation rather than the statistical one cited. For, given the statistical belief and the outcome of Zee's exposure, what became plausible was some such law as this: all persons in physical condition like that of Zee at the time of their inoculation are rendered immune to the disease. It would seem odd if Zee disbelieved this and yet believed himself to have been immunized by inoculation; that would be outright defiance of induction. The recommended gen-

eralization admittedly suffers from vagueness for want of spelling
out what it is to be in physical condition like that of Zee. Still,
viewing the explanation this way makes it seem closer to ful-
filling our criterion.

We are disinclined to accept purely statistical explanations as
the last word on any matter. Such statistics as that 93 percent
of those who are inoculated become immune may be enough to
relieve curiosity in a case like the one above, but the intellect
balks at supposing that there could be no further explanation
that would account for why just those who were inoculated but
not immunized were in fact not immunized. We would expect
there to be some explanation for the exceptions, though we
might think that finding one was too much to hope for. True,
there are the irreducibly statistical hypotheses of quantum mechanics; but then we laymen find it hard to see them as explanatory.

An explanation is subject, we have seen, to at least the following three requirements. First, the explanation, when taken in the
suitably inclusive way, must imply the thing it was meant to
explain. Second, it must meet the two antitriviality stipulations.
And third, of course, it is acceptable only to the extent that it is
a plausible hypothesis. At this point Virtues I through VI play
their part. Ad hoc hypotheses, hypotheses that are unfalsifiable
because they yield no predictions—all such are to be shunned
in explanations as elsewhere.

Explanation can be an important means of supporting a
hypothesis. Confirmation of a hypothesis consists in verifying
its consequences, but we do well also to look in the other direction
and consider what could imply the hypothesis. For the hypothesis
inherits the full support of any belief that implies it. Thus it
is wise and customary to seek explanation not only for what
we already believe true, but also for unproved hypotheses. We
are rightly wary of beliefs for which no explanation could be
envisaged.

In general we tend to believe not only that explanations exist,
but that ones that would enlighten us exist. We believe, for
instance, that crimes have solutions. Solutions to crimes give
explanations for them, explanations that meet special requirements: they identify the implicated persons, the methods used
in the crime, and often the motives. Now just as some unsolved
crimes have only a small number of reasonable suspects, it often
happens that when we look for an explanation we reasonably

believe that it will be found within certain narrow limits. We believe that one of some small number of conceivable explanations must be right. In this situation, elimination of some of the possibilities increases the plausibility of those that remain. Sometimes even an explanation that was initially held to be implausible is accepted because it explains something that can be explained in no other conceivable way. Men have been hanged for want of plausible alternatives.

We see therefore that there can be mutual reinforcement between an explanation and what it explains. Not only does a supposed truth gain credibility if we can think of something that would explain it, but also conversely: an explanation gains credibility if it accounts for something we suppose to be true. Sometimes an explanation has no evidence at all to support it apart from the fact that it would, if true, explain something we want explained; and it can draw high credibility from this source alone. If we think of an ingenious way of explaining one of Harry Houdini's baffling escapes—some ingenious contrivance of sliding panels or a severed link—we are apt to accept it simply because we doubt that any other reasonable contrivance could have done the trick. Such argument from exclusion, or from want of evident alternatives, often inspires more confidence than it deserves; but still it has its place. It seems fair to say that any statement is entitled to at least some increment of credibility from the mere circumstance that it would, if true, explain something for which we have found no other explanation. This accounts, in particular, for the interest in mechanical simulation of physiological or mental processes. The mere fact that the machine produces similar results gives some presumption that the details of the hidden mechanism in the brain or body are significantly similar to the machine.

We must be wary, as Molière taught us, of explanations couched in fancy language. It is a basic maxim for serious thought that whatever there is to be said can, through perseverence, be said clearly. Something that persistently resists clear expression, far from meriting reverence for its profundity, merits suspicion. Pressing the question "What does this really say?" can reveal that the fancy language masked a featureless face. We should also be wary of explanations that seem to work too well, explanations that seem always to be available. If we can conceive of no way of testing "Whatever God wills happens," then we give no explanation when we call something God's will. If we can conceive of no way of testing which of a person's acts spring from his unconscious desires, then we give no explanation of a person's act when we lay it to his unconscious desires. If a hypothesis is untestable, it cannot tell us anything.

We should be wary of explanations that appeal to motives and character traits. Witness what might be offered as explanations for a man's electing to dedicate himself to some self-sacrificing career in which he serves the needs of others. It might be that his concern for other persons was so overwhelming that such a career was all he could consider, so we might explain his choice in terms of his love for his fellow man. But it might also be that he suffered from some neurosis that made him afraid to think of himself in what are for most people ordinary ways; so we might explain his choice as a neurotic one. These would seem as diverse as two explanations could be. Yet it is no stretch of the imagination to suppose that both might be correct. What is more, there need not have been anything in the man's psychological history that would justify our saying that the one had more to do with his choice than the other. It is a sad fact about our views of others (and perhaps of ourselves) that we are inclined to adopt in such a case just the explanation that fits our prejudices. If we like the man we cite his spirit of humanity; if we dislike him we cite his neurosis. This is sad because our prejudice is thereby reinforced and our vision narrowed, yet without our having accepted anything false, and so without our story's being liable to refutation.

Attributing motives and character traits to persons as aids in explaining their behavior is legitimate only when such attributions can be regarded as hypotheses open to question in the light of further information. Talk about motives and character traits being as loose as it often is, we may too easily become intransigent about an attribution once it has been made. The belief that someone is a selfish scoundrel, once adopted, may be defended in the face of almost anything he is seen to do. This, we recall from Chapter V, is true to an extent of any hypothesis if we are willing to make enough adjustments in our other beliefs, but beyond a point it is folly to do this. Even Virtue I, conservatism, will be on the side of jettisoning a belief when the alternative is to make whole deckloads of one's other beliefs walk the plank. The particular danger in attributions of motives and character traits is the possibility of defending them in almost any circumstances without doing much violence to our other beliefs. The danger, in short, is lack of Virtue IV, refutability.

Where this virtue is wanting, it becomes questionable how much content the attributions have. Characterological attributions to groups of persons as well as to individuals can be offered as deep truths and as justifications for attitudes and actions even when they are empty.

The moral to draw from these reflections is not, however, that motives and character traits should never be attributed. The psychology of motives and character traits is in its infancy, but there is no call to conspire in arresting its development. The moral to draw is just that the question "What does this really say?" is a good one to ask, especially when attributing motives and character traits.

We have seen cases where the search for explanation was mainly one for laws. There the data, for example about lunar position, were sometimes too obvious to be mentioned, except for purposes of showing how our explanation applied. In the explanations that people give of what they and others do, the situation tends to be reversed; specific statements are given—like "because he loved her" and "because I was angry at you for not letting me go to the doubleheader"—and there is normally no appearance of any lawlike sentence. This is because in such cases there is little doubt about what the relevant lawlike sentences would be. They would be on the order of "In normal circumstances one does what one wants," together with commonly accepted generalizations about particular attitudes and emotions. These are vague when spelled out; it is not really even clear what it comes to to say that a person *wants* to do something. Equally vague, generally, are the explanations people offer of their own behavior. These are often intended less as explanations than as reports of what one had in mind when making some decision. What would be a boon for explanations of behavior would be sharper psychological concepts.

Explanations of behavior commonly appeal to purpose. "Why did you telephone Umberto, of all people?" "So as to ask him about some of his political promises." "But why by phone instead of letter?" "So as to get his impromptu reaction." Explanations by appeal to purpose are called *teleological*. Often they are just what we want and were asking for; but they are explanations in a sense of the word that is very different from what we have been discussing up to now. Teleological explanations differ conspicuously, certainly, from causal laws; for they run to specificity rather than generality, as remarked, and furthermore they cite future purposes rather than past causes. Teleological explanation does not take the place of causal explanation. Having wanted and got a teleological explanation of someone's act, that is, having got an account of his purposes, we could still be interested in a causal explanation of how he came to have those purposes.

Somewhat puzzlingly, teleological explanations are not confined to explanations of purposive behavior. One hears teleological explanations that relate to biological function or preservation of species. Consider the question "Why do we have eyes?" and the imaginable answer "To see with." Consider "Why does this tree deposit some of its seeds so far from its trunk?" and the response "So that they can receive sunlight." Such explanations, like the teleological explanations of behavior, appeal to goals without any overt appeal to general truths. And, as the second illustration is meant to show, such explanations can be informative.

If the question had been "For what are our eyes used?," the same answer "To see with," would have been all the more appropriate. What would have been requested is a statement of function, not an explanation in our sense. This is a possible way of viewing teleological explanations in biology—not as explanations properly speaking, but as statements of function, offered in answer to "Why" questions that are themselves only disguised inquiries into function and not really requests for explanation.

We must pause, however, to examine an alternative treatment of such questions and answers. One might defend a vaguely statistical hypothesis to the effect that a creature is likelier to have a trait if it is conducive to the survival of his species. A weak explanation of our having eyes, then, in our regular sense of the term "explanation," could be held to consist in that tacit statistical hypothesis, plus the explicit functional answer "To see with," plus an unstated commonplace about the utility of sight for survival. The more serious example about the tree and its seeds would be accommodated in the same way.

We reflected earlier that for any hypothesis adduced by way of explanation we can ask, if we please, an explanation in turn. The vague statistical hypothesis above is one that emphatically invites explanation in turn. And such an ulterior explanation has indeed been proposed from time to time down the ages, in the form of the hypothesis of a divine plan. One of the faults of this hypothesis, however, is that it raises more pressing questions than it settles: What plan? How implemented? Another fault is that, being untestable, it tells us nothing; whatever is found to happen counts *ipso facto* as part of the plan. It is like the suspect hypothesis that we noted earlier: God's will. Darwin expressed the criticism thus: "It is so easy to hide our ignorance under such expressions as the 'plan of creation' . . . and to think that we give an explanation when we only restate a fact."[1]

Darwin himself offered a more serious ulterior hypothesis to explain why creatures tend to have traits conducive to survival. It was the hypothesis of natural selection, or survival of the fittest. Organisms show chance variations over the generations because of a process of genetic "mutation" (which was for Darwin just an unexplained fact). These new traits then tend to be handed down to further generations if they are conducive 'to survival; otherwise they tend to disappear because their carriers tend to die before reproducing. Thus species that survive are to be expected to exhibit traits conducive to that survival, as with our tree. Darwin's is an exemplary explanatory hypothesis, which appeals to plausible and independently discoverable processes. It became, of course, the cornerstone of modern biology. And it reduces the teleological explanations of biology sweepingly and systematically to explanations in a stricter sense of the word.

[1] Charles Darwin, *The Origin of Species* (London: 1859; 1st ed.), p. 408.

EXERCISES

1. Aiming for maximum variety among your examples, cite several good explanations and tell why they are good ones. By way of contrast, find or invent some poor explanations and tell why they are poor.

2. Find some examples like the Houdini one in which argument from exclusion seems to yield an acceptable explanation.

3. Manny grumbles "It must be a woman driver" whenever he sees an inept maneuver on the road. When, as often happens, it becomes apparent that the offending driver is not in fact a woman, Manny shifts his grumble to "He drives just like a woman." Discuss, and find further illustrations of thinking like Manny's.

4. Focus on some beliefs that you hold about various character traits of particular persons. For each of these beliefs sketch your support and describe what in the way of fresh findings would lead you to alter the belief.

Chapter IX

Persuasion
and Evaluation

We noted two basic purposes of language: getting others to do what we want them to, and learning from others what we want to know. The former of these purposes is often concisely served by a command or request; this commonly suffices if the one party loves or fears the other, or is happy to do small favors simply to ease social tensions or out of the kindness of his heart. In more awkward cases, the use of language in getting someone to do what we want him to is more elaborate. We undertake to persuade him that he will gain by doing the thing. We may persuade him of this by offers or threats. Also we may persuade him of advantages that would redound to him quite apart from any reward or reprisal on our part. Our problem in this case is to implant a belief in him. Here, then, is a purpose neatly converse to what we saw as a second basic purpose of language: that of learning something from others. Here the purpose is to get others to learn something.

Such, perhaps, under

> The jungle law
> Of tooth and claw
> That still held sway
> In man's primeval day,

was the original point of convincing others: to get others to do what was wanted. Teaching, thus motivated, can diverge sharply from the effort to inculcate one's beliefs in others, since we may get others to do things by implanting beliefs which we do not share. This is the utility of lying.

Happily, these deceitful measures are often inhibited by another ancient force, the force for truthfulness that we speculated on in Chapter IV. This force has prevailed more in some circles than in others; and it has prevailed fully, we are glad to say, in the circle to which this little book is addressed. For this sincere circle, the business of convincing others reduces neatly to the business of convincing others of one's own beliefs.

The purpose of getting people to do things justifies indeed no general effort to propagate our beliefs, even with deception set aside; for many of our beliefs simply do not bear on people's action. Still, many of us are happy to go on propagating our beliefs even when nothing is to be gained but the sharing of them. Like Chaucer's clerk, we gladly teach. To convince others of one's beliefs may simply be faced as a general objective, then, with or without ulterior motive. Such is the proper business of argument.

To maintain our beliefs properly even for home consumption we must attend closely to how they are supported. A healthy garden of beliefs requires well-nourished roots and tireless pruning. When we want to get a belief of ours to flourish in someone else's garden, the question of support is doubled: we have to consider first what support sufficed for it at home and then how much of the same is ready for it in the new setting.

Beliefs typically rest, to change the figure, on further beliefs. Some of these supporting beliefs may record the reports of observations, but often in making a belief acceptable to someone there is no need to cite observations. He may already share enough of the other supporting beliefs so that merely calling attention to some of the relevant connections will suffice to convince him. For instance W. W. Skeat, dean of English etymologists, wrote in his dictionary that he saw no plausible etymological link between *heaven* and its German translation *Himmel*. Nor did he venture any between *ever* and its German translation *immer*. Yet he surely knew perfectly well, not on the Germanic side but on the Celtic side, that *m* regularly changes to *v* in certain circumstances. One wonders whether a mere simultaneous glimpse of these three separately familiar matters might not have sufficed to make him believe that *heaven* and *Himmel* were etymologically connected after all.[1]

We convince someone of something by appealing to beliefs he already holds and by combining these to induce further beliefs in him, step by step, until the belief we wanted finally to inculcate in him is inculcated. The most striking examples of such arguments, no doubt, are mathematical. The beliefs we invoke at the beginning of such an argument may be self-evident truths: this was Euclid's way. But they need not be, so long as they are beliefs our friend already holds.

It may happen for instance that our friend, like Gilbert and Sullivan's modern major general, knows and admires the Pythagorean theorem. It says that the area of the square built upon the hypotenuse of a right triangle is equal to the sum of the areas of the squares built on the other two sides of the triangle. Seeing his admiration for this little theorem, we eagerly ply him with further good news in the same vein. We tell him that the theorem holds not just for squares but for all shapes equally. As long as the three sides of a right triangle constitute corresponding parts of three figures that are alike in shape, the area of the one figure will be the sum of the areas of the other two. Our friend, though visibly gladdened by this generalization of the Pythagorean theorem, is mathematician enough to ask to see the proof. Following in ancient footsteps, we cite another theorem, one having to do with the proportions between the areas of similar figures. This theorem says that if you measure the distance between any two points in one figure and then measure the distance between the corresponding points in another figure of like shape, the areas of the two figures will be related as the squares of the two distances. This theorem is perhaps not quite self-evident. Moreover, we ourselves perhaps do not happen to see quite how to prove it from self-evident beginnings; but happily we are not required to, for we find that our friend already believes it. Also, as we know, he believes the original Pythagorean theorem; and happily, having these two theorems now in mind, he sees also—what is perhaps not quite self-evident either—that our generalization of the Pythagorean theorem follows from the two. Our task of convincing our friend is now accomplished, and we are free to change the subject or to go about our business.

[1] We are indebted to Conrad M. Arensberg for bringing the three together for us.

We see here a difference between persuading and training. If we were instructing a pupil in the generalization of the Pythagorean theorem, and not merely regaling a friend, we would press the pupil regarding the preliminary theorem about proportions between areas of similar figures. We would not merely acknowledge his acceptance of it and go on from there. Part of our responsibility to our pupil is to school him in critical and rigorous thinking. We would ask him to prove that preliminary theorem. If he failed, we would prove it for him, even at the cost of some interim homework on our own part.

In an effort merely to persuade someone of something, on the other hand, it would be presumptuous to argue for any preliminaries that he already accepts. We do well in such a case merely to seek a basis of shared beliefs broad enough to support the belief that we are trying to put over. We do well to appeal to a common ground of beliefs which are no more particular and detailed than necessary for agreement. Such is the *maxim of shallow analysis*. It is no guide for teachers, we saw, and it is a poor maxim also when we are assessing our own beliefs. But it is a good maxim in argument, for it minimizes effort for ourselves and boredom for our audience.

In mathematical arguments, and likewise in the Skeat example, the supporting beliefs directly appealed to do not include reports of observation. On the other hand some arguments do drive us back to observational data. Now it should be noticed that the appeal to our observations in the argumental situation, where we are out to convince others, is a weaker instrument than it was when we merely ministered to our own beliefs. The difference is that when we report an observation, we have the observation and others have only our testimony. Our observation reaches the other persons at one remove, and that one remove rubs out the guarantee that may be seen as stamped on observation. Thus, even though we have solid ground for a belief, there is this rub when we try to convince others. The distinctive trait of observation is, as we noted earlier, that all witnesses agree. One way to make up the difference in decisiveness between our observation and our reporting of it, then, is to get the skeptic to repeat the observation with his own eyes. But sometimes this is a nuisance that the skeptic will not take on, and sometimes, as in the case of a murder or collision, the observation just does not bear relevant repetition.

Much hinges, therefore, on the credibility of our testimony. In

Chapter IV we noted what considerations might reasonably govern our credence of other people's testimony; and these apply now in reverse. For one thing there was the question of possible ulterior motives, or conflict of interest. Our testimony gains in credibility insofar as we appear to have nothing substantial to gain by being believed, and perhaps even something to lose. Our testimony gains in credibility also insofar as we have succeeded on past occasions in showing ourselves coolly judicious and moderately skeptical. And our testimony gains in credibility most of all if our past behavior has made it evident that we never attempt to inculcate any beliefs but our own. Just as each of us forms hypotheses about the reliability and credibility of others, so do others form such hypotheses about us; and the best way to insure favorable ones is to earn them.

We have been reflecting on the credibility of our testimony specifically in the domain of observation reports, where testimony is often essential and irreducible because of unrepeatable observations. But trustworthiness has immense practical value elsewhere too, if only as a labor saver; for it implements the maxim of shallow analysis. The more honest and intelligent we are thought to be, the less supporting argument we are apt to have to produce in order to convince someone of something. In an extreme, indeed, such a reputation can be harmful to oneself and others, lulling both parties into inattentiveness to evidence.

Let us now sum up something of the nature of argument. To convince someone of something we work back to beliefs he already holds and argue from them as premises. Perhaps we also insinuate some supporting beliefs, as needed further premises. We may succeed in insinuating a supporting belief simply by stating it, or we may be called on to offer support for it in turn. We aim, of course, for supporting beliefs that the person is readier to adopt than the thing we are trying finally to convince him of. His readiness to adopt what we put to him will depend partly on its intrinsic plausibility and partly on his confidence in us. If in particular a proffered belief is a mere report of our observation, he may accept it routinely; for in accepting it he has to trust only our memory and our moral character and not our judgment. If on the other hand he balks even at our observation report, we may try to get him to do the observing.

Often there is also a negative element to contend with: actual disbelief of some of the needed premises. For dealing with this kind of resistance there are two strategies, which are the same as the strategies for broaching the walls of a mediaeval city: overwhelming and undermining. To overwhelm, we adduce such abundant considerations in favor of our thesis that we end up convincing the man in spite of his conflicting belief. He simply gives up the conflicting belief, deciding that there must have been something wrong with whatever evidence he once supposed he had for it. To undermine, on the other hand, we directly challenge his conflicting belief. If he meets the challenge by mustering an argument in defense of that belief, then we attack the weakest of the supporting beliefs on which he rests that argument. Commonly, of course, a combined strategy of overwhelming and undermining is best of all.

Thus, suppose we are defending our political candidate against one of his critics. Our case for him is that he will reduce taxes, reduce street crime, and put an end to the bribery that is corrupting the urban renewal program. But the critic questions this third premise, citing the candidate's long association with a real-estate broker who was implicated in the bribery scandals. If we adopt the strategy of overwhelming, we do not deny the alleged association. We perhaps adduce other evidence—from the candidate's activities in the city council—which tends to show that he is nevertheless a force against corruption in urban renewal. Also we apply ourselves more energetically to the other two premises. We cite impressive evidence of the candidate's record of motions and votes on budgetary questions, and also impressive figures of the drop in the crime rate when the candidate was head of the Citizens' Committee. Perhaps for good measure we also throw in and defend a new premise: that he will improve the schools.

If, on the other hand, we adopt the strategy of undermining, we produce reasons for believing that the candidate's association with the corrupt broker had after all been neither friendly nor profitable, and that the rumors to the contrary were traceable to the broker himself. If finally we combine both strategies, and do so with a good show of evidence at each point, our candidate may presently count his former critic among his staunch supporters.

It is agreeable to note that in the use of the strategy of undermining there is occasionally a repercussion. What may occasionally happen is that our challenge to the conflicting belief is met by so able a defense that we find ourselves persuaded. In this event we are led to give up the very belief that we originally sought to propagate. This is the best outcome of all, if we like surprises and are bent on learning things. This is a time when the second of the basic purposes of language noted earlier has unexpectedly been fulfilled: the purpose of learning from others.

The desire to be right and the desire to have been right are two desires, and the sooner we separate them the better off we are. The desire to be right is the thirst for truth. On all counts, both practical and theoretical, there is nothing but good to be said for it. The desire to have been right, on the other hand, is the pride that goeth before a fall. It stands in the way of our seeing we were wrong, and thus blocks the progress of our knowledge. Incidentally it plays hob with our credibility rating.

The desire to be right is the unimpeachable member of the pair, but even here a word of caution is in order: being right is not always a sign of right reason, or of being reasonable. One might succeed in drawing two to a flush, but it is still bad poker. The best strategy does not win every time; what makes it best is just that in the long run it promises most.

We would rather, of course, be right than reasonable. We would like to get the flush. But what course could one hope to find that would guarantee being always right? What makes the best strategy reasonable is that it does cause us to be right—our beliefs to be true—more generally than alternative strategies do. When the evidence available points the wrong way, away from the truth, the reasonable person is wrong along with it.

To learn to distinguish the plausible from the implausible is to develop one part of wisdom; it leads as well as anything can toward true belief. But wisdom's better part bids us remain aware that we have less than the whole truth about even those matters we understand best. Such awareness can never be misplaced, since "the whole truth" about anything is but a fanciful ideal.

We speculated that a primeval purpose of trying to convince people of things was to get them to do what we want them to. We went on to reflect that this harsh purpose was gratefully softened as the world improved; sincerity flowered, and with it the urge to share beliefs for sharing's sake. There is a domain, however, where the practical purpose, the influencing of action, continues to stand forth in very nearly its primeval starkness. This is the domain of values. It is an imposing domain, but a brief postscript is all that we can accord it within the scope of this book.

To say that an act is good, or right, comes near to commanding it outright. To say that an object is good, or beautiful, comes near to urging that it be coveted. We are apt to support such a commendation of an act or object by adducing reasons, as we might for any belief; but our having begun our discourse with a value statement is already almost a declaration that our subsequent argument has the practical purpose of inducing our listener to perform the act or covet the object. Whether our desire for this result is itself traceable to selfish motives, as in the case of a salesman, or to generous ones is of course a further and independent question.

The evaluative beliefs are the beliefs about what is good, bad, beautiful, right, obligatory, or simply preferable to something else. Beliefs can be evaluative without lending themselves to ready expression in such terms; and, even more important, many beliefs whose articulation invites such terms can be unpacked in ways which avoid them. Attempts to draw a sharp line between beliefs, or sentences, that evaluate and those that do not have been mainly grievous. Like other distinctions we have met, this one is best seen as admitting of shades.

Concern with the grounds of evaluative belief raises fewer new issues than one might expect. It is largely a matter of criteria: to the extent that we can find suitable criteria for a given belief, we can reduce the question of its acceptability to the question whether those criteria are fulfilled. This is of course true of any belief. But it is especially important for evaluative belief, because the criteria that we resort to tend to be less evaluative than the original evaluative belief itself.

Thus whether Lefty ought to be the team's shortstop, left-handedness notwithstanding, is likely to be seen as a question of what alignment makes the team strongest. Whether the melons in the crate are good ones might be settled by attending to their firmness, coloring, and size, or by eating them. Whether there ought to be an airport close to town can be seen as turning in part upon the facts about sonic booms. Evaluations of various teaching procedures can hinge upon current theories in the psychology of learning.

It was obvious that we were evaluating in Chapter V when we declared what were to be regarded as Virtues—and what as vices —in the winning and winnowing of hypotheses. The criterion there, which made certain traits of hypotheses count as Virtues, was predictive efficacy. The Virtues distinguished those hypotheses that prove on the whole to be richest in their verifiable predictions.

For some sorts of evaluation, criteria are hard to specify:

judging works of art, for example. Critics give reasons for their judgments, and, for the most part, the better a critic the more plausibly he is able to support his evaluations. But criteria may vary from critic to critic, and some of these differences may seem basic enough to be regarded as differences in taste. *De gustibus,* we may in that case be told, *non disputandum.* Still, what has been said in foregoing pages regarding the support of beliefs applies in particular to aesthetic judgments insofar as they can be supported at all, or can be used in support of further judgments.

Interlinking of beliefs is more conspicuous in questions of right and wrong than in aesthetics. An argument for the rightness or wrongness of a type of action may lean heavily on the consequences that that action may have. We think it wrong to drop heavy objects from high rooftops because serious injury might result. Sometimes, rather than looking to consequences, we appeal directly to some sort of rule or principle: that breaking promises is wrong, that creativity is to be encouraged, that persons are to be treated as ends rather than as means. There is interplay between the two kinds of considerations; we appraise an action's consequences in the light of rules or principles, and we appraise rules or principles in the light of the expected consequences of their acceptance. In questions of right and wrong the principles do, nevertheless, tend to come first; the word "principle" means substantially that. Disagreements about principles can stubbornly resist rational resolution. The person who thinks that animal life is to be more highly valued than human amusement is unlikely to be swayed by the arguments of the modern huntsman, and conversely.

Happily, such differences of principle are not very common. As the philosopher Hume saw, men have common basic sentiments. Why, then, do we disagree as much as we do in our moral evaluations? Why do bills rarely receive unanimous support or rejection in legislatures? Part of the answer lies in the workings of self-interest, prejudice, and other psychological pressures. These forces make people disagree with one another as to what is right and what is wrong, and even make it difficult, sometimes, for a man to maintain consistency in his own moral evaluations. However, since the rightness or wrongness of an act hinges so much on its expected consequences, we may be sure that one very important reason why people disagree in their moral evaluations is simply that they differ also in their knowledge or belief regarding other matters. In a person's web of beliefs there is no strand that may not help support some value judgment.

1. Emphasizing the rationale involved, describe some cases in which you succeeded in changing another person's beliefs and some cases in which another person succeeded in changing yours.

2. Set down some of your own evaluative beliefs, specifying as well as you can the criteria that seem suitable to each one. Include some beliefs that appear to rest on rules or principles.

3. Elaborate on the observation that caution or certainty about a belief reflects belief about that belief. Discuss the support appropriate to such second-order beliefs.

4. Another distinction that admits of shades rather than a sharp line is the one between beliefs and attitudes. Develop and illustrate this thought.

5. In evaluating human actions one must not forget that there can be diverse explanations for a person's having done something. Develop this thought, drawing on what we observed in Chapter VIII.

Suggested Readings

Relatively elementary:

✓A. J. Ayer, *The Problem of Knowledge.* Baltimore: Penguin, 1956.

P. W. Bridgman, *The Logic of Modern Physics.* New York: Macmillan, 1927.

J. Bronowski, *The Common Sense of Science.* Cambridge: Harvard, 1953.

N. R. Campbell, *What Is Science?* New York: Dover, 1952.

J. B. Conant, *Science and Common Sense.* New Haven: Yale, 1951.

Pierre Duhem, *The Aim and Structure of Physical Theory.* New York: Atheneum, 1962. (French edition 1914.)

Philipp Frank, *Modern Science and Its Philosophy.* Cambridge: Harvard, 1950.

Martin Gardner, *Fads and Fallacies.* New York: Dover, 1957.

✓C. G. Hempel, *Philosophy of Natural Science.* Englewood Cliffs, N.J.: Prentice-Hall, 1966.

✓T. S. Kuhn, *The Structure of Scientific Revolutions.* Chicago: University of Chicago Press, 1962.

M. K. Munitz, *Space, Time, and Creation.* Glencoe: Free Press, 1957.

C. S. Peirce, *Essays in the Philosophy of Science* (V. Tomas, ed.). New York: Liberal Arts, 1957.

W. V. Quine, *Methods of Logic.* New York: Holt, 1959.

Hans Reichenbach, *The Rise of Scientific Philosophy.* Berkeley: University of California Press, 1951.

Bertrand Russell, *Human Knowledge.* New York: Simon and Schuster, 1948.

✓Gilbert Ryle, *Dilemmas.* Cambridge: Cambridge University Press, 1954.

Israel Scheffler, *Conditions of Knowledge.* Chicago: Scott-Foresman, 1965.

Israel Scheffler, *Science and Subjectivity.* New York: Bobbs-Merrill, 1967.

Suggested Readings

Somewhat more technical:

— Nelson Goodman, *Fact, Fiction, and Forecast*. New York: Bobbs-Merrill, 1965.
— N. R. Hanson, *Patterns of Discovery*. Cambridge: Cambridge University Press, 1958.
C. G. Hempel, *Aspects of Scientific Explanation*. New York: Free Press, 1965.
David Hume, *Treatise of Human Nature*. Oxford: Clarendon Press, 1896. (First published 1739.)
Leonard Linsky (ed.), *Semantics and the Philosophy of Language*. Urbana: University of Illinois Press, 1952.
W. V. Quine, *Word and Object*. Cambridge: M.I.T., 1960.
— Israel Scheffler, *The Anatomy of Inquiry*. New York: Knopf, 1963.